THE EVERYTHING® KIDS' FOOTBALL BOOK

8th Edition

All-Time Greats, Legendary Teams, and Today's Favorite Players—with Tips on Playing Like a Pro

Greg Jacobs

Adams Media

New York London Toronto Sydney New Delhi

Adams Media
An Imprint of Simon & Schuster, LLC
100 Technology Center Drive
Stoughton, Massachusetts 02072

An Everything® Series Book.

Everything® and everything.com® are registered trademarks of Simon & Schuster, LLC.

This Adams Media trade paperback edition September 2024
First Adams Media trade paperback edition July 2008

ADAMS MEDIA and colophon are registered trademarks of Simon & Schuster, LLC.

Simon & Schuster: Celebrating 100 Years of Publishing in 2024

For information about special discounts for bulk purchases, please contact Simon & Schuster Special Sales at 1-866-506-1949 or business@simonandschuster.com.

The Simon & Schuster Speakers Bureau can bring authors to your live event. For more information or to book an event, contact the Simon & Schuster Speakers Bureau at 1-866-248-3049 or visit our website at www.simonspeakers.com.

Interior layout by Erin Alexander
Illustrations by Jim Steck
Puzzles by Beth L. Blair

Manufactured in Canada

Printed in Montmagny, Quebec, Canada by Marquis Imprimeur Inc.

10 9 8 7 6 5 4 3 2 1

ISBN 978-1-5072-2288-1
ISBN 978-1-5072-2289-8 (ebook)

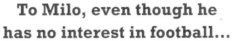

**To Milo, even though he
has no interest in football...**

Acknowledgments

I only get a few lines here, so I can't fully express my appreciation to all of these folks. But copious thanks anyway to: Bart and Mary Ann Jacobs, the late Jack Soete, Peter Cashwell, Clint Alexander, Keith Johnson, Brad Jones, Taaj Davis, Gene Ware, David Glover, Brad "Spider" Caldwell, the Penn State football program, Andrea Bell, Kerry Smith, Grace Freedson, Joe Nero, and Henry Sydnor. And, to my wife and sidekick, Burrito Girl, a.k.a. Shari Jacobs, who lets me watch football on the big-screen TV all season. She's the best.

 Contents

Chapter 6

Offensive Football / 79

Chapter 7

Defensive Football / 97

Chapter 8

Super Fans / 115

Chapter 9

Behind the Scenes / 123

★ Introduction

Whether you're a huge football fan or just starting to learn about the game, this book is perfect for you! If you're new to football, Chapter 1 has the answers to all your questions. And if you want to play football without all the tackling, Chapter 1 will also introduce you to flag football, which is a safer version of the game but just as fun! Both longtime and new fans will enjoy the two chapters on professional football and the one on college football. Look for "Football Great" boxes, which feature mini profiles of pro and college stars from the early days to today.

You probably watch high school games in your area or watch college and pro games on TV. But did you know that the players and coaches spend weeks working hard and preparing before the game? Two chapters will give you a peek into what goes on behind the scenes: Chapter 5 is about high school football, and Chapter 9 talks about the important people who help make the game great. You'll learn how scouts and statisticians help teams win and help fans understand the game better. Plus, there's advice on how to start and run your very own fantasy football league in Chapter 8!

If you already know the basics of football or want to learn more about the "Xs and Os," there are two chapters just for you: one about offense and one about defense. No matter how much you play, watch, or read about football, this book hopes to teach you something new and exciting about the game.

Throughout the book, you'll find player and team stats, cool trivia, and ideas for drills and games you can try with your friends. And best of all, each chapter is full of fun, football-themed puzzles. Are you ready to play? **Let's go!**

Playing the Game

Where Did Football Come From?

In most parts of the world besides here in the United States, when people talk about football, they mean the game we call soccer. People have played games with balls and goals for a very long time. At least five hundred years ago in England, football, or the game we call soccer, developed. In soccer, players try to put a round ball into a goal without using their hands. But when Americans talk about football, we mean the game you play with a brown oval-shaped ball.

In the early 1800s, players at the Rugby School in England began playing a different version of soccer. They picked up the ball and ran with it to the goal, which was against the rules. Some teams liked to play against the Rugby School—they just tackled whoever picked up the ball! Other teams liked the old way better. This led to two different games: rugby, where players could run with the ball, and soccer, where they couldn't.

Americans picked up the game of rugby, but every team wanted to play by different rules. In the late 1800s, several colleges and athletic clubs in America played games similar to rugby. East Coast universities such as Princeton, Rutgers, Harvard, and Yale eventually got together to try to standardize the rules.

By the early 1900s, American rugby had changed enough that you probably could have recognized the game as football. Every play was a running play. Blockers (without much padding) slammed into each other as hard as they could. There were so many injuries, in fact, that many people tried to ban the sport. President Theodore Roosevelt asked Yale athletic director Walter Camp to lead a group that would make football a more exciting and less dangerous game than had been played before. Camp came up with new rules, like having eleven players on each team and needing to gain yards for a first down. Most importantly, Camp invented the forward pass.

College Football

College football in the early 1900s was dominated by the schools that are now part of the Ivy League. Other schools had a hard time winning against them, and it wasn't until 1912 that a school outside of the Ivy League won a national championship. Back then, college football was more popular than professional football. People loved watching college teams play, and many colleges across the country started their own football teams. The games played on New Year's Day, called bowl games, were the highlight of each season.

In the 1920s, football became even more popular. Colleges from all over the country had football teams, and professional teams started playing in the Midwest. Both college and professional football were well-known and had lots of fans. However, football didn't become as big as it is today until after the Great Depression and World War II.

Find the Flag

Can you find the seven times the word FLAG is hidden in this game of flag football?

Football GREAT

George "Papa Bear" Halas

George Halas played for the company football team at a starch plant in Decatur, Illinois, in the 1910s. Under his leadership, his company team became the Decatur Staleys of the National Football League. He moved the team to Chicago and renamed it the Bears in 1922. Halas ran pretty much the entire Bears organization: He played, he coached, he recruited, and he even sold tickets! In recognition of Papa Bear's contributions to his team and to the NFL, the Bears uniforms have sometimes shown Halas's initials, GSH, on the sleeve.

TV Makes Football Popular

By the end of the 1950s, most families had a TV at home. Televised football made the game even more popular. The Super Bowl, first played in 1967, became the most important sporting event in America, and millions of people watched it every year.

Today, you'll see both college and pro football on TV—college on Saturday, pro on Sunday. Many college teams and almost all pro teams sell out their stadiums every week. High schools and youth leagues stage games each week, giving more people a chance to play the game.

Rules of the Game

Football can seem really complicated with all its rules. The official rulebook is more than two hundred pages long! But you don't need to know everything to start playing. Just learn the basics, and the rest will make sense as you go along.

The Simple Rules

A football game consists of four quarters, two in each half. In high school, the quarters are twelve minutes long. In college and in the NFL, the quarters are fifteen minutes long. Whichever team has more points at the end of the four quarters wins. If the game is tied, the teams usually play overtime. A football field has a 100-yard playing field and two 10-yard end zones. The offense scores points by getting the ball into the other team's end zone, and the defense protects its end zone by keeping the other team as far away from it as possible.

Scoring

There are four ways for the offense to score.

1. **Touchdown—6 points.** Run the ball into the end zone or catch the ball in the end zone.
2. **Extra point—1 point.** After a touchdown, the offense gets one free play. If they kick the ball through the goalposts, they get 1 more point.
3. **Two-point conversion—2 points.** Instead of kicking an extra point after a touchdown, the offense can try to get the ball into the end zone. If they succeed on that play, they get 2 more points.
4. **Field goal—3 points.** Kick the ball through the goalposts.

Offensive Rules

A play starts when the center hikes, or "snaps," the ball between his legs to the quarterback. Until the snap, most of the offensive players must not move. Usually the quarterback does one of two things after the snap:

- He gives the ball to a running back, who runs with the ball behind his blockers.
- He drops back to try to pass the ball to a receiver while the blockers protect him.

In a running play, all the offensive players are supposed to block. This means they push the defensive players out of the way so the running back has room to run. On a passing play, receivers run down the field, trying to get open so they can catch a pass. The linemen stay near the quarterback to block the defenders trying to sack him. If a receiver catches the ball, he can keep running. However, if the ball hits the ground before anyone catches it, that's called an incomplete pass. The offense has to try again from the same spot.

WORDS TO KNOW

PLAY: In soccer or basketball, once the game starts, it keeps going for a long time. In football, once someone is tackled, the game stops for everyone to line up and start again. A play is the action that happens after the ball is hiked and before someone is tackled. Plays can usually be described as passing plays or running plays.

SACK: When the defense tackles the quarterback before he has a chance to pass the ball, that's called a sack. Bruce Smith, who played most of his career for the Buffalo Bills, sacked the quarterback two hundred times and holds the all-time NFL record.

OFFENSE AND DEFENSE: The team of eleven players that controls the ball is the offense. They try to run or pass the ball down the field toward the end zone. The team of eleven players without the ball is the defense. They try to tackle the offensive player with the ball, and they try to knock down or intercept passes.

WORDS TO KNOW

HOLDING: Neither offensive nor defensive players are ever allowed to hold a player who doesn't have the ball. This means no jersey grabbing, hugging, or tackling. Holding usually results in a 10-yard penalty. (Of course, the defense is supposed to do these things to the person who's carrying the ball!)

PASS INTERFERENCE: When a pass is in the air, the defense can't make contact with the receivers. If they do, the penalty is called pass interference, and it usually costs 15 yards—sometimes even more in the NFL.

FUN FACT

The Defense Can Score Too

Sometimes the offense can't move forward because the defense tackles the ballcarrier behind the spot where they started the play. If the defense pushes the offense so far back that the ballcarrier is tackled in the end zone, the team on defense gets 2 points. This play is called a safety.

Whether they run or pass, the offense has to keep moving if they want to keep the ball. They have four plays, called downs, to move 10 yards on the field. If they make the 10 yards, they are awarded a first down, and they keep the ball. If they don't get those 10 yards, then the defense gets the ball.

Fourth down is the offense's last chance to keep the ball. Often, the offense realizes that they're probably not going to get a first down. So they can choose to punt: They kick the ball to the other end of the field. The other team then gets the ball, but way farther back than if the offense hadn't punted.

Defensive Rules

The defense, like the offense, is allowed to put eleven players on the field. Unlike the offense, the defense can move around before the snap. On running plays, defensive players are allowed to collide with blockers to knock them out of the way while they try to tackle the ballcarrier. On passing plays, though, there are stricter rules. No one is allowed to interfere with a receiver trying to catch the ball.

The defense's job is to keep the offense from getting a first down. They can do even better, though, by forcing a turnover. If a runner drops the ball, which is called a fumble, the defense can pick it up and keep the ball. If the defense catches a pass, that's called an interception, and the defense gets to keep the ball.

You Can Play Too

Most college and professional football players are well over 6 feet tall and weigh more than 200 pounds. You'd never be able to tackle them, even if you and all of your friends tried together. But that doesn't mean you can't play football. Kids' football leagues make sure that everyone, no matter how big or small, can play.

One way of making a game competitive is to be sure that all the players are about the same size. The country's oldest and best-known youth football organization, Pop Warner, takes this approach. Kids as young as five years old can join a team, and there are divisions for kids up to sixteen years old.

Pop Warner teams play tackle football in helmets and pads, and the rules are adjusted for the ages of the players. (For example, the five- to seven-year-olds can play on a smaller 80-yard field.) Games are just like high school games, with ten- to twelve-minute quarters. However, unlike at higher levels of football, in Pop Warner, every player gets to participate in every game.

Pop Warner teams compete in local leagues, usually playing about six to eight games each fall. But before playing a game, they start with practice. Each year, players spend a week or so conditioning and then learning the fundamentals of blocking and tackling before they even put on pads. Then, more practices in pads are required. By the time the team is ready for the first game, everyone on the team knows what to do. Football is a complicated game, so the practice time pays off when it's time to compete.

The Pop Warner teams are divided into associations of a few local teams each. The winner of an association can advance to the playoffs, with each round consisting of the winners of a larger area. With enough wins, a team can advance to the national tournament. There, the best teams in the country from each age group play off to crown a national champion.

Of course, there are other youth football organizations besides Pop Warner. In some areas, each city sponsors teams. There are also independent leagues, Boys & Girls Clubs of America leagues, county leagues, and even leagues of elementary or middle school teams. Most of these leagues match players of the same age and size, provide equipment and coaching, and play a weekly schedule.

Football GREAT

Glenn Scobey "Pop" Warner

Pop Warner was a standout football player at Cornell University who went on to coach college football for forty-five years, starting in 1895. He is the one who had the idea for players to wear numbers, and he also introduced the huddle and many other common football techniques. He supported a youth football league in Philadelphia in the 1930s. The league eventually became the Pop Warner Conference.

For Experts Only: The Strangest Rule

All football experts know that if the player catching a kickoff or a punt waves his arm over his head, it's called a fair catch, and the kicking team has to give him space to catch the ball. But do you know what a fair catch kick is? In the NFL and in high school, the receiving team is allowed to try a field goal from the spot of the fair catch, without anyone trying to block the kick. There's no snap—the kicker puts the ball on a tee and kicks. The kick is worth 3 points if it goes through the uprights.

Skills for Every Type of Player

One of the great things about football is that almost anyone can find a position that they're good at, especially on a kids' team. The three most important features of a football player are strength, speed, and football smarts. At your age, these skills are best developed by playing a lot. Older players—starting in high school—put themselves through complex weightlifting or speed training programs. That's important for older players, but until you get to high school, just play as much as you can, and you'll find that your body grows into its skills.

If you are one of the fastest in your class, then you should try playing receiver or cornerback. If you're one of the biggest or strongest, then you could be a linebacker, a lineman, or a running back. And if you can throw the ball and make quick decisions, you might be an excellent quarterback.

Some people grow stronger, faster, or smarter than others. We can't all have the body of T.J. Watt or the intelligence of Richard Sherman. You might think you're too slow to be a receiver. But as your legs get longer and your muscles get bigger, your speed will improve. If you know exactly where to throw the ball but your arm is too weak to get the ball there, don't give up the thought of being a quarterback. Keep practicing for a few years, and you could find that all of a sudden, your throws are right on target. On that same note, remember that the folks you play against are also not fully grown. If you're the biggest player on your team, you might think that you should stick to playing offensive line or running back. What happens, though, if next year your teammates are all your size or bigger? There's no reason you shouldn't try playing every position, learning the necessary skills, and having fun.

Playing It Safe

Playing any sport, especially contact sports like football, soccer, or basketball, means risking injury, including concussions. A concussion is an injury to the head, particularly the brain, frequently involving a loss of consciousness and dizziness.

Most of the hits to your head playing a sport will just end up bruising on the surface. The skull does a really good job protecting your brain. But sometimes the hit is so hard, your brain gets injured. That's a concussion, and you have to look out for it.

Some signs of a concussion include:

- Vomiting
- Dizziness or walking unsteadily
- Different-sized pupils or pupils that don't react to light
- Talking that makes no sense
- Losing consciousness

If you hit your head, it could be a serious injury. Make sure you tell an adult right away. You will be evaluated to see if you might have had a concussion. Your football team or association will have rules covering when you will be able to play again. It's important to avoid playing until you're cleared.

Football Is a Team Game

The number one goal in football is for the team to win. That might mean you have to play your second-favorite position. Your coaches know what's best, and you have to trust them to balance the goals of playing everyone and winning as well.

Woofball

Use a light color marker to highlight all the letters that are not W, F, or B. Read the highlighted letters to find the answer to the riddle!

What do you get when you cross a dog with a football player?

F	A	B	B	F	W
B	W	F	G	W	F
O	F	F	B	F	W
W	B	L	W	B	D
F	E	F	W	N	W
B	F	W	F	F	B
F	B	R	W	F	E
C	W	F	W	F	F
W	E	B	F	I	B
F	B	W	V	F	W
W	E	B	W	B	R

USA Football

The NFL created an organization called USA Football that supports all youth football leagues. You can go to its site (www.usafootball.com) for information on a league close to you, training sessions, health and safety in football, or even how to become a football official.

Safety First

It's not smart to play full-contact football without pads, especially if some of the players are smaller than others. Blocking and tackling are certainly an important part of the official game of football, but you can design games that focus on other football skills by making up different ways to "tackle" and "block."

You might even have to wait your turn to play. If you aren't in the game and your team scores a touchdown, cheer with them just as if you had been playing. Everyone will see what a good sport you are and what a great, positive attitude you have, even when you don't get to do exactly what you want. Maybe later in the game you'll get your chance. Don't you hope that when you score, your teammates celebrate with you?

Backyard Football

Organized youth football leagues only play one game per week, but you want to play more football than that, right? While a league is the only way to get involved in tackle football with pads and helmets, there's no reason you can't play a simpler version of the game on a playground or in your backyard.

Probably the most common way to play football without tackling is to play touch football. When someone touches the ballcarrier with both hands, the play ends. No equipment at all is required (other than a ball, of course). You can play anywhere—just put some cones or backpacks on the ground to show where the end zones are.

Flag Football

Another substitute for tackle football is flag football. In flag football, everyone wears a loose belt with ribbons, called flags, on it. Instead of tackling the player with the ball, you pull the flags off the ballcarrier's belt. Flag football can be played by people of all ages and with lots of different rules. In the leagues sponsored by the NFL, teams of five players play on a 50-yard field. In another version of flag football that is played on college campuses, teams of seven players play on an 80-yard field.

Flag football leagues for kids are as common as baseball leagues. Schools, community centers, sports clubs, and even the NFL sponsor leagues and teams. It's not a contact sport—in many leagues, the offense not only isn't allowed to block; they're not even allowed to be in the path of a defender trying to get the ballcarrier's flags! So, for flag football, it's not as important as in tackle football to be sure all players are of similar size. Most teams are sorted by age group, like an "under twelve years old" team or a "fourth- and fifth-grade" team. And no equipment is necessary beyond flags and a football—no helmets or pads.

Flag football leagues have their own set of rules that have evolved from touch football. The most common rules include:

- **First and cone:** A cone is placed at midfield, or maybe several cones are placed every 20 yards. Passing the next cone earns a first down, whether that means gaining 1 yard or 19 yards.
- **Pass rush:** The referee places a beanbag 10 yards from the line of scrimmage. Only defenders who begin behind the beanbag may cross the line of scrimmage during the play. This gives the quarterback time to throw...but not too much time!
- **Extra points:** Most flag football doesn't include the kicking game. After a touchdown, teams can choose to try to score from, say, the 3-yard line for 1 point or from the 10-yard line for 2 points.

No Warding!

All a defender has to do to "tackle" a ballcarrier in flag football is to pull a flag out of a belt. It seems like the ballcarrier should just slap the defender's hand away. Nope! That's called *warding,* and it usually results in a 5-yard penalty. The ballcarrier is allowed to shimmy their hips to make a defender miss, but they can't use their hands!

Many flag football leagues, especially below high school–age leagues, include both boys and girls. Even though most boys eventually grow bigger and stronger than most girls, in elementary and middle school, it's just as often the *girls* who are bigger, stronger, and faster than boys of the same age. So girls and boys can compete on the same teams. There are also leagues just for girls and women, including high school, college, and community-sponsored adult teams.

CHAIN GANG: In an official football game, a 10-yard chain is carried along the sideline to determine the yardage necessary to make a first down. The people who hold the chain in the right spot for a measurement after each play are called the chain gang.

What about Blocking?

You can avoid tackling people in your backyard by playing touch or flag football, but how do you block? If everyone's about the same size, and if most of you have learned proper blocking form, you might just block normally. But a more common method, often used in flag football, is to block like you play defense in basketball: Shuffle your feet and establish a position so that no one can get by you. Then, if someone runs you over, they've committed a foul (like charging in basketball).

You can eliminate the blocking parts of the game altogether. Unless you have a huge number of players, make the rules so the offense usually passes, and make it difficult to rush the quarterback. Here are some ideas:

- **Use a rush count.** This means that anyone who wants to rush the quarterback has to stay at the line of scrimmage and count out loud: "1-Mississippi, 2-Mississippi..." The rusher can cross the line after "5-Mississippi."
- **Make every two completions worth a first down.** You don't have someone to measure yards on the playground anyway. Backward passes, or passes thrown behind the line of scrimmage, don't count. This way, the offense is still allowed to run, but they're usually going to pass in order to keep getting first downs.
- **Don't let the quarterback run with the ball unless the defense crosses the line of scrimmage.** Just like you can let the defense blitz once every four downs, you can let the quarterback run once every four downs.
- **Only let defenders who lined up 10 yards behind the line of scrimmage rush the quarterback.** This rule makes the game a bit more like real football, but it still gives the quarterback enough time to throw passes.

Way to Play

Use the key to decode the football player's answer to the reporter's question.

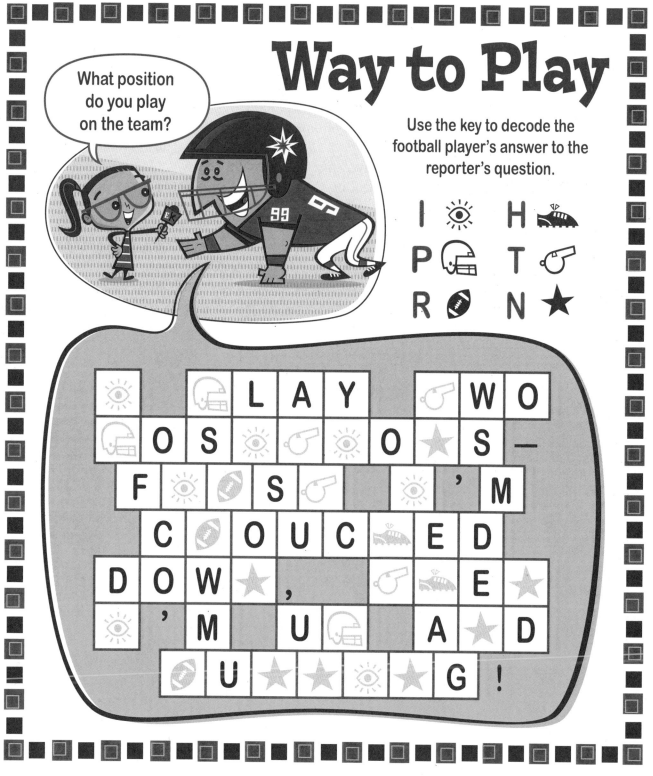

Backyard Football for Just a Few Players

Flag and touch football work best with teams of five to seven players. But what if you don't have enough for teams that big? Or what if you have an odd number of players so that the teams don't divide evenly?

Dealing with an odd number of players is simple. Make the person who can throw best the steady quarterback. This player plays quarterback for both teams. If several people want to play quarterback, then rotate who gets to be the steady QB every four touchdowns or so.

With teams of three or four, you can use a small field. Put a cone or something at midfield for the first-down marker. Make the rule that you have four plays to get past the cone for a first down, then you have four more plays to score a touchdown.

Kicking Without Goalposts

Unless you are a true football fanatic, you probably don't have goalposts in your backyard. You'll need to change the rule about extra points. Give the team that scores a touchdown one free play. They have the choice of trying for 1 or 2 points:

- If they spot the ball at the 3-yard line, they get 1 point for getting into the end zone.
- If they instead spot the ball at the 10-yard line, they get 2 points for getting into the end zone.

Field goals are more difficult. You can make a rule that field goals don't count in your game, so everyone has to try for touchdowns. Or you can put a cone 10 or 20 yards from the end zone, and the team who gets past this cone can choose to take 3 points for kicking a field goal. Or award a field goal to a team that can kick the ball so it lands in a small circle in the end zone. Be creative. You can find all kinds of ways to make field goals part of the game, even if you can't kick it through the uprights.

Competitive Football Skill Games

Sometimes you just can't get a real game going when you don't have a lot of people to play. You can still have some football fun, though. Try playing some games similar to drills at a football practice. Here are some ideas:

- **Man-to-man coverage:** The quarterback says "Hike," and a receiver runs out for a pass. One defender tries to intercept or knock down the pass. The receiver gets 1 point for a complete pass, and the defender gets 2 points for an incompletion. Make a time limit of, say, three seconds for the quarterback to release the ball.

- **Target accuracy game:** Set up a bunch of targets—long cones, chairs, or tree trunks work fine. Assign each target a point value, with closer or bigger targets worth less. Put a bunch of footballs in front of a quarterback. Someone says "Go!" and times thirty seconds. The quarterback earns points by hitting the targets with the ball. Everyone else races to return the thrown balls to the quarterback. Then it's someone else's turn. See who can get the most points in thirty seconds.

- **Pass pattern game:** This one takes a few more people. Use three receivers and two defenders. The receivers go out for a pass, but they all have to start and stay on only one side of the field. The quarterback has to throw the ball within three seconds. The receiver is down right after catching the ball. Give the offense 1 point for each yard they get on a completion; give the defense 2 points for an incompletion. You can adjust the scoring depending on the size of the field and the skill of the defenders.

CHAPTER 2

The National Football League

A Brief History of the NFL

In the early days of American football, the best-known teams were college teams, mainly from the Northeast. But in many manufacturing towns of the Midwest, teams from city athletic clubs played against one another, and lots of people came to watch them play. Competition was fierce, and in order to gain an edge against other cities, clubs began paying money to recruit the best players.

In 1920, fourteen teams made up the American Professional Football Association, which was renamed the National Football League two years later. *National* was a funny name for the league since the teams were only from a small part of the country.

The All-America Football Conference

The NFL had a very hard time surviving in the 1930s and 1940s. In the Great Depression of the 1930s, many families didn't have enough money to feed themselves, let alone to pay to watch football games. The economy improved in the early 1940s, but the best football players had to fight in World War II. When the war ended in 1945, huge numbers of athletic young men were returning from military service. People had extra money to spend. The NFL's owners were looking forward to big profits.

But in 1946, a competing league began to play: the All-America Football Conference (AAFC). The AAFC put teams in many NFL cities, like Chicago and New York.

The NFL refused even to acknowledge the existence of this new league. In fact, when a major sports magazine included the AAFC in a football preview issue, the NFL banned that magazine's writers from its games! But there was no denying that the AAFC was popular. More people were going to AAFC games than to NFL games.

The American Professional Football Association	
These were the fourteen teams that started the association that became the NFL. Only one of the teams was located outside the Midwest, and only two of these franchises are still playing today:	
Akron Pros	Dayton Triangles
Buffalo All-Americans	Decatur Staleys (still playing as the Chicago Bears)
Canton Bulldogs	Detroit Heralds
Chicago Cardinals (still playing as the Arizona Cardinals)	Hammond Pros
Chicago Tigers	Muncie Flyers
Cleveland Tigers	Rochester Jeffersons
Columbus Panhandles	Rock Island Independents

Paul Brown and his scouting staff with the Cleveland Browns did better than any other team in recruiting the most talented young players, and so they ended up dominating the AAFC during its four years of play. The fact that the Browns were so much better than any other team led to the league's downfall, and it played its last game in 1949. Three teams from the AAFC—the 49ers, the Browns, and the Baltimore Colts—joined the NFL the next year, while the other teams ceased to exist. It was another decade before the NFL faced another serious challenge from a new football league.

Another New League and Expansion

Professional football reached new heights of popularity in the 1960s. TV networks showed games on Sunday afternoons, exposing more of the country to the game. Pro football finally started to become as important and as well known as college football.

The surge in pro football's popularity made room for other teams. But the successful NFL owners were hesitant to

The First Professional Football Player

In 1892, the Allegheny Athletic Association paid Pudge Heffelfinger $500 to play in a game against the Pittsburgh Athletic Club. That amount of money is equivalent to about $10,000 today. That sounds like a lot, but the minimum NFL salary in 2024 works out to $38,000 per game, and most players make a lot more.

The First African-American NFL Head Coach

Fritz Pollard was both a star halfback at Brown University and a chemistry major. After graduation, Pollard played and coached professional football for eighteen years. He was player-coach for the Akron Pros in 1921. Soon, though, white supremacist owners led by George Marshall kicked Pollard and other Black players out of the NFL. But Pollard continued to coach successfully, mostly with all-Black barnstorming teams like the Chicago Black Hawks.

Ending Racial Segregation

It was the AAFC, not the NFL, that first allowed Black players to play after World War II. Future Hall of Famers Marion Motley and Bill Willis helped the Cleveland Browns win their first-ever AAFC game in 1946.

add franchises. So a number of businesspeople, led by Lamar Hunt, formed a new league: the American Football League.

Expansion

The NFL, of course, did not like competition. It finally agreed to add a few more teams: The Vikings, Cowboys, Falcons, and Saints all joined the NFL in the 1960s. But the AFL expanded too, adding the Miami Dolphins and the Cincinnati Bengals. Teams were offering more and more money to players, trying to get them to switch leagues.

Eventually, in 1970, the AFL and the NFL merged to become two conferences in a single National Football League. There were ten AFL teams and sixteen NFL teams, so as part of the merger, the Baltimore Colts, Cleveland Browns, and Pittsburgh Steelers agreed to join AFL teams in the new American Football Conference, the AFC. The remaining thirteen teams formed the National Football Conference, the NFC.

Bigger and Bigger and Bigger

The NFL was not done expanding. In 1976, the Seattle Seahawks and the Tampa Bay Buccaneers joined the league, the Carolina Panthers and Jacksonville Jaguars joined in 1995, and the Houston Texans were created in 2002. But expansion was about more than just adding new teams in new cities. After the merger, the NFL set about to grow in every possible way.

For a long time before 1960, NFL teams played twelve games in their regular season. That number increased to fourteen games per season in 1961. In 1978, the sixteen-game schedule began. And since 2021, the NFL has played seventeen games each season.

Starting with the merger in 1970, the playoffs were expanded to ten teams: six division winners and four wild card teams. In 1990, two more wild card teams allowed twelve teams in the playoffs, and two more were added in 2020. More playoff games meant more TV money and more big events. The NFL season, which used to be completely over in December, stretched into early February.

More Teams, More Games, More Playoffs

NFL expansion created new and more dedicated fans. Every city wanted a team, but the NFL couldn't just add an unlimited number of teams. Cities started convincing owners to move their teams. The Oakland Raiders moved to Los Angeles in 1982, moved back to Oakland in 1995, and became the Las Vegas Raiders in 2020. Before the 1984 season, the Baltimore Colts moved to Indianapolis in the middle of the night. The St. Louis Cardinals became the Arizona Cardinals in 1988. St. Louis got a new team in 1995 when the Rams relocated there, but in 2016, the team moved to Los Angeles along with the (previously named) San Diego Chargers. The Houston Oilers moved to Tennessee to become the Titans in 1997. The Cleveland Browns moved to Baltimore in 1995 to become the Ravens, and a new Browns team was created in 1999.

Why did all these teams move? In most cases, the new city offered the owner a brand-new stadium and lots of money. These new stadiums were more comfortable than the old ones and included more luxury boxes. The new cities had plenty of folks willing to pay enormous amounts of money for season tickets, and plenty of rich people or companies ready to pay for the luxury boxes. Owners found that simply by threatening to move to a new city, their original city would often build a new stadium just to keep the team from moving. In 2024, twenty-two of the NFL's thirty-two teams played in a stadium that had been built

WORDS TO KNOW

THE MERGER: Officially, the AFL merged with the NFL in 1970, even though they had played championship games since the 1966 season. You will often hear broadcasters refer to events "since the merger." Though team and individual statistics before 1970 are official and do count in the record books, the year of the merger represents when the NFL started to resemble the league you watch today.

WILD CARD: Before 1970, the only teams in the playoffs were the division winners. In the 1970 season, the two teams in each conference with the best records that were not division winners were invited to the playoffs. These teams played each other in the wild card game. The winner of that game advanced to play a division winner. In the opening weekend of today's playoffs, three wild card teams in each conference travel to play three division-winning teams.

in this century; all but three played in a stadium that was probably built in your parents' lifetime.

The NFL Championship Game

Before 1933, the NFL held no playoffs, just a regular season. The champion was the team with the best record. In 1932, though, Chicago and Portsmouth were tied for first place. The teams played a one-game playoff to determine the champion. This game was so popular that, starting in 1933, the NFL divided its teams into two conferences and planned an NFL championship game between the conference winners. An additional divisional playoff game was played if two teams tied for the top spot in a division. Winning the NFL championship was, for forty-five years, the greatest honor in professional football. The Super Bowl (see Chapter 3) didn't exist until the 1966 season.

The NFL kept exactly this format all the way through 1966. In 1967, it divided each conference into two divisions. The division winners played off to determine a conference champion, and the conference champions played in the NFL championship game.

WORDS TO KNOW

HOME FIELD ADVANTAGE: The seven teams in each conference that make the playoffs are ranked based on their regular season record and tiebreakers. In every playoff game (except the Super Bowl), the team with the better ranking gets to play at their home field. The home team doesn't have to travel, and they usually play better in front of their own fans. In fact, the home team wins about 60 percent of the time. Interestingly, in 2020, games were played in front of either no fans or very few fans because of the pandemic. And that year the home teams won only about 50 percent of the time.

AFC East	AFC West	AFC North	AFC South
New England Patriots	Denver Broncos	Cincinnati Bengals	Indianapolis Colts
New York Jets	Kansas City Chiefs	Pittsburgh Steelers	Tennessee Titans
Miami Dolphins	Los Angeles Chargers	Baltimore Ravens	Jacksonville Jaguars
Buffalo Bills	Las Vegas Raiders	Cleveland Browns	Houston Texans

NFC East	NFC West	NFC North	NFC South
Philadelphia Eagles	Seattle Seahawks	Green Bay Packers	Carolina Panthers
Dallas Cowboys	San Francisco 49ers	Chicago Bears	New Orleans Saints
New York Giants	Arizona Cardinals	Detroit Lions	Atlanta Falcons
Washington Commanders	Los Angeles Rams	Minnesota Vikings	Tampa Bay Buccaneers

Who Are These Teams, Anyway?

The NFL's thirty-two teams are divided into two conferences: the American Football Conference (AFC) and the National Football Conference (NFC). These conferences can be traced back in league history to the AFL-NFL merger in 1970. The AFC consists mainly of old AFL teams, and the NFC consists mainly of original NFL teams. The NFL's two conferences are each broken into four divisions, with four teams in each division.

How Do You Figure Out a Team's Schedule?

Each team plays seventeen regular season games. With thirty-two teams, it's not possible for a team to play every other team in a season. Instead, each team plays a schedule that depends on what division they're in, with most of the opponents changing from year to year because division matchups vary.

For example, here's how the NFC North's Green Bay Packers schedule broke down in 2023:

- Two games each against the other teams in their division: So they played the Bears twice, the Lions twice, and the Vikings twice.

Arena Football— in 1932!

The NFL scheduled a one-game playoff between Chicago and Portsmouth to be played at Wrigley Field in Chicago in December. A giant snowstorm hit the Chicago area the week before the game, and then it got cold—really, really cold. So the NFL decided to play the game inside! The teams played on a special 80-yard field indoors at Chicago Stadium, the same building where the Chicago Blackhawks hockey team and, later, the Chicago Bulls basketball team played.

Women's Football Alliance

The Women's Football Alliance is a semiprofessional league with three divisions and many dozens of teams around the country. It's full-contact tackle football in pads, for women. *Semiprofessional* means that while players are paid, they also hold regular full-time jobs. For example, the quarterback of the 2022 national champion Mile High Blaze, Kimberly Santistevan, is a firefighter and a preschool teacher.

The Raiders' Coaching Carousel

Most head coaches are allowed a few years to try to build a winning football team. When a coach stays with a team for a long time, he provides stability, discipline, and a winning program that the players like. However, the Oakland Raiders (now Las Vegas Raiders) have had fourteen head coaches since the turn of the century! In contrast, the New England Patriots have had only two head coaches during that time.

- One game each against the teams in the NFC South: the Panthers, Saints, Falcons, and Buccaneers.
- One game each against the teams in the AFC West: the Chiefs, Raiders, Chargers, and Broncos.
- Since the Packers finished third in their division (NFC North) in 2022, in 2023 they played two more games against other NFC teams that also came in third in their division: the Rams and the Giants.
- One additional game against another AFC team that also finished in third place the previous year—in this case, the Steelers. In 2023, this seventeenth game was a home game for the AFC team. In 2024, it will be a home game for the NFC.

The other NFC and AFC divisions the Packers match up against rotate each year.

The Bosses

Have you ever heard TV reporters talk about a team's power structure? They don't mean the offensive line. Though the players play the games, there's a whole group of people on every team who determine which players play and how they play, including the coach, the general manager, and the owner.

The Coach

The head coach is responsible for preparing his team for each game. In the game itself, the head coach makes strategic decisions, like whether to punt or to try for a first down. NFL football is so complicated that a head coach can't run everything alone. The head coach hires a large number of assistants, who take charge of smaller parts of the job. For example, the linebacker coach teaches the linebackers how to play their positions, and the defensive coordinator coaches the defense and is in charge of each week's defensive game plan.

Coaching seems pretty easy. It's the players who have to run and tackle, and the coaches just watch, right? But coaching is exhausting in a different way. Coaches watch game videos all the time. They look at their next opponent, trying to find weaknesses. They look at their own games, evaluate players, and figure out how to make their own guys more successful. Coaches prepare for practice just like a teacher prepares for class. Once practice is over, the coach goes right back to preparing.

A winning NFL team requires great players as well as great coaching. It's not always fair to judge a coach as good or bad based on his record in one or two seasons. Yet it's reasonable to say that the best coaches are those who have led their teams to the playoffs many times over the years. For example, one of the best NFL coaches today is Andy Reid of the Kansas City Chiefs. Reid coached the Philadelphia Eagles for fourteen years, taking the Eagles to the playoffs in nine of those seasons and winning 58 percent of his games. Even successful coaches get fired—the Eagles let Reid go after a losing season in 2012, but the Chiefs picked him up the next year. Under Reid's leadership, the Chiefs became a Super Bowl team.

The General Manager (GM)

The coaches figure out what to do with their players. But a coach can't just ask any old player to join his team. A team must first sign that player to a contract and agree to pay him a salary. It is the general manager's job to find and sign players to fill out the team.

Each team is only allowed to spend a certain amount of money each year. This "salary cap" means that if a star player wants a lot of money, the general manager, or GM, either needs

Football GREAT

Coach Bill Belichick

Belichick began his NFL coaching career with the Detroit Lions and Denver Broncos. However, his first successful stint came under head coach Bill Parcells with the New York Giants, with whom he won two Super Bowls as the team's defensive coordinator. In 2000, he became the head coach of the New England Patriots, leading them to the playoffs in eighteen of twenty-two years, as well as nine Super Bowl appearances and six Super Bowl victories. He won seventeen division titles, by far more than any coach in NFL history. His 302 wins as a head coach are behind only George Halas and Don Shula for the most ever.

Brush Up

This coach is giving one of his players a compliment — or is he?
To find out what the coach is saying, you must write all the   letters from
the scattered pieces into their proper spaces in the grid.
Hint: Try matching the pattern of the orange boxes.

to let that player go to another team, get rid of another player, or pay other team members less. If a GM wants a player who is already signed to a contract by another team, the GM has to make a trade. Perhaps the most visible part of a GM's job comes on draft day when each team's GM takes turns picking former college players to be part of their teams. Figuring out which players to draft requires serious scouting and research. The NFL draft is shown on national TV so that fans everywhere can see the decisions each team makes right away.

The Owners

Head coaches and GMs worked for many years at lower-level football jobs. These folks proved their worth before being hired to such an important position. No matter how good coaches or GMs become, though, they're not going to work their way up to become owners. The owner of a franchise is simply the person who bought the team. Football knowledge isn't required to buy an NFL team, but having a lot of money is. For example, Dan Snyder bought the Washington team in 1999 for $800 million. In 2023, he sold the team for $6 billion.

An ideal owner buys the team, hires a strong GM and an outstanding coach, and lets *them* make all the football decisions. If the GM or the coach isn't performing well, it is the owner alone who has the power to fire them. That's often a difficult decision for an owner. If the team didn't make the playoffs this year, is it because the GM did a poor job of obtaining players? Were the players good enough but poorly coached? Or was it a really good team that just hit a few bad breaks and will be very good next year? It's usually hard to tell the difference. Since it's easier to fire the coach than to fire all the players, the coach is often the one who pays the price for a bad season.

Shopping for Players?
Some coaches are willing to put in the extra work to gain the extra control of being able to sign as well as coach players. As legendary coach Bill Parcells once said, "If they want you to cook the dinner, at least they ought to let you shop for some of the groceries."

How Long Do Coaches Last?
Washington has had ten different head coaches in the twenty-first century. On the other hand, the Pittsburgh Steelers are only on their third coach since the AFL-NFL merger in 1970.

Be a Part of the Action

Most NFL stadiums have room for about seventy thousand people. Being one of those seventy thousand, all cheering at the top of their lungs for the home team to win, is an experience that you will treasure for a long time. If you get a chance to go, be sure to look around you, see everything that is happening, and really savor the trip.

Getting Tickets

Ticket prices for NFL games are very, very high. It costs about $370 for just one ticket to one game, and that's for an average advance ticket in an average-priced stadium. A last-minute ticket to a New England Patriots game costs more than $750!

Most NFL tickets are sold as season tickets. To get a season ticket, you pay the team an upfront "personal seat license" fee, you pay the team for ten tickets, and you get to sit in the same seat for all eight or nine regular season home games and the two preseason home games.

At the Game

Before you go, ask someone or look online for advice about getting to the stadium. With seventy thousand people trying to cram into one building, crowds can get huge and lines can get long. Find out where to park and if there's a better way to get to the stadium than by car. Also, read up on stadium rules about what you can bring with you. No backpacks are allowed at NFL games, but you can bring a small, clear-sided bag with things like water, sunscreen, a poncho, a hat, and sunglasses.

The game will definitely be exciting, causing you and all the fans to cheer, yell, scream, and jump out of your seats. That's exactly what's supposed to happen! Be sure to be

TAILGATING: A tailgate party is a picnic in the stadium parking lot before a game. This can be as simple as eating some sandwiches out of a cooler while sitting on the back of your car. Elaborate tailgaters bring lawn chairs, big grills, and four-course meals. Part of the fun is being with all the other tailgating fans of your team. Bring extra food to share, and you'll meet some interesting folks!

Find the Football

Find the one time that FOOTBALL is spelled correctly. Look up and down, side to side, and backward.

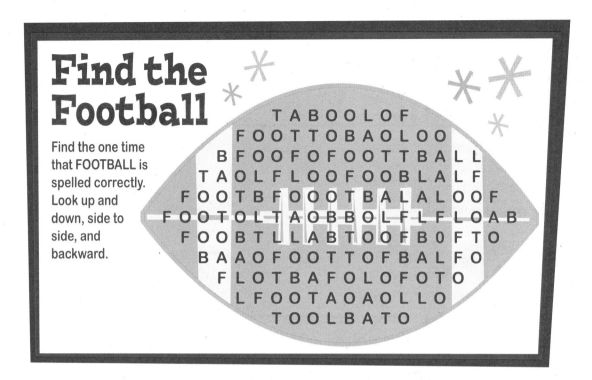

```
     T A B O O L O F
   F O O T T O B A O L O O
  B F O O F O F O O T T B A L L
 T A O L F L O O F O O B L A L F
F O O T B F O O O T B A L A L O O F
F O O T O L T A O B B O L F L F L O A B
F O O B T L L A B T O O F B 0 F T O
 B A A O F O O T T O F B A L F O
 F L O T B A F O L O F O T O
  L F O O T A O A O L L O
     T O O L B A T O
```

considerate of others while you're cheering, though. You—and the other fans—don't need to use foul language, throw things, or be obnoxious to fans of the visiting team. Cheer as loud as you can for your team, but don't be rude and ruin someone else's experience.

Watch for parts of the game you can't see on TV. You'll notice parts of football that the narrow TV screen can't show you. Before the game and during halftime, walk around. Most stadiums have murals, statues, or wall hangings honoring the team's history. Talk to some fans in the concession line and find out where they're from, what they know about the team, and how long they've been fans. You're at an NFL game, one of the greatest possible American cultural experiences—make the most of it!

Fractured Football

The linebacker hit the football so hard it was broken in half! Which two pieces will fit together to make one complete ball?

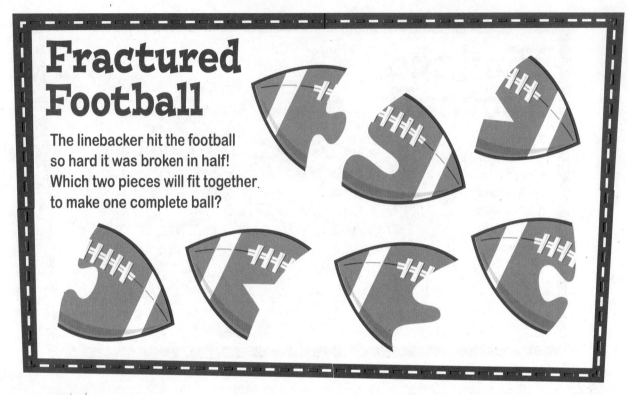

Monday Night Football

In the 1960s and 1970s, no more than two games were shown on TV each Sunday. In 1970, ABC started showing one game every Monday night, using their best announcers and lots of cameras and graphics to produce a big show. Monday Night Football (MNF) lasted until 2005 on ABC, and every week, it was one of the top ten most-watched TV shows. Now, MNF is on ESPN networks.

If You Can't Go

You can watch virtually any NFL game on TV if you can't go to the game. Watching on TV is a less intense experience, but it is a lot more convenient (and a lot cheaper too). Near a city, the home team's games will almost always be shown on local network channels. If you want to watch an out-of-town team, you may have to watch on a paid service. A satellite or streaming package allows you to watch every NFL game on Sunday afternoons.

CHAPTER **3**

The Super Bowl

The Origins of the Super Bowl

In the 1960s, when the rivalry between the NFL and the upstart AFL was at its peak, Chiefs owner Lamar Hunt and Cowboys owner Tex Schramm led a campaign to merge the two leagues into one big National Football League. They agreed to play a championship game between the AFL and NFL winners starting after the 1966 season.

A few years after Hunt and Schramm's agreement, most people thought the NFL was a far better league than the AFL. In the first two AFL-NFL championship games, the NFL's Green Bay Packers soundly defeated their AFL opponents. NFL fans and owners wondered whether agreeing to play against such bad teams had been a smart move. But in the third AFL-NFL championship game (in what is now known as Super Bowl III), the AFL's New York Jets beat the NFL's Baltimore Colts by 9 points, even though the Colts had been favored to win by more than two touchdowns. The AFL's Kansas City Chiefs blew out the NFL's Minnesota Vikings in Super Bowl IV after the 1969 season. When it came time in 1970 for the leagues to actually merge (see Chapter 2), they did so as equals, because the AFL had proved that they could win Super Bowls.

Football GREAT

The Undefeated 1972 Dolphins

In 1972, the Miami Dolphins became the first team to win every game in a season. The team capped its 14-0 regular season with three postseason victories, including a 14-7 victory over Washington in Super Bowl VII. Members of the 1972 Dolphins still celebrate together each season after the last undefeated team loses a game.

Playoffs

How does a team get to the Super Bowl? After the seventeen-game season, the best teams get to play in the playoffs. In playoff games, whichever team wins gets to play again the next week, and the losing team is done for the season. The last playoff game is the Super Bowl, and the winning team is the NFL champion.

A total of fourteen of the thirty-two teams—seven in each conference—make the playoffs. Figuring out which teams get into the playoffs isn't easy.

Here are the guidelines:

- The winning team in each division makes the playoffs.
- In each conference, the three teams with the best records that aren't division winners also make the playoffs. These are called wild card teams.

Once the playoff teams are determined, the playoff schedule is set. The first weekend after the regular season is wild card weekend. The wild card teams play against the division-winning teams, except for the team in each conference with the best record—they earn a bye, meaning they automatically advance to the divisional round.

The winners from wild card weekend play in the divisional playoff round the next week. Then come the conference championship games, after which only two teams are left—the AFC champion and the NFC champion. These are the teams that go to the Super Bowl.

Sometimes the conference championship games are more exciting, creating more lasting memories, than the Super Bowl itself. A team who loses the Super Bowl still *made it* to the Super Bowl. But usually, history only remembers who won the conference championship. Many of these games have come down to the last, tension-filled moments—moments so famous that they have two-word names.

The Catch

At the end of the 1981 season, the Cowboys and the 49ers played the NFC championship game to determine who would meet the upstart Bengals in Super Bowl XVI. The Cowboys were favored to win; they were "America's team," while 49ers

FUN FACT

Tiebreakers

The hard part of figuring out who's in the playoffs comes when teams finish the season with the same record. The NFL tiebreaker rules are quite complicated. Games within a division and games between teams in the same conference are most important when determining who wins a tiebreaker. You can read the details at www.nfl.com.

Football GREAT

John Madden

You may know John Madden from his NFL video game, but that's not the only reason he's in the Hall of Fame. Madden was drafted by the Philadelphia Eagles in 1958, but his career was cut short by injury. He first became well known in the NFL as head coach of the Oakland Raiders teams of the 1970s. His Raiders won Super Bowl XI after the 1976 season. When he retired in 1979, he was hired by CBS as a color commentator.

quarterback Joe Montana was still new and unproven. The Cowboys led with fifty-one seconds left. On third down from the 6-yard line, Montana seemed about to be sacked. He scrambled back and to his right and threw the ball high out of the back of the end zone. But not too high for receiver Dwight Clark! Clark jumped as high as a track star, getting his fingertips to the ball, and dropping both feet in bounds at the back of the end zone for the winning touchdown. That play flipped the balance of power in the NFC for a decade—the 49ers were the best team of the 1980s, while the Cowboys didn't win a playoff game between 1983 and 1991.

The Drive

Another memorable conference championship moment occurred in the AFC championship game after the 1986 season. That contest pitted the Cleveland Browns, who had never been to a Super Bowl, against the Denver Broncos. With five minutes left in the game and the Browns ahead by 7, the Broncos muffed the kickoff and had to start from the 2-yard line. Even with eighty thousand Cleveland fans screaming at him, quarterback John Elway led the Broncos all the way to the end zone, using fifteen plays and all but thirty-seven seconds of the clock to tie the game. Decades later, Elway's march is still known simply as "The Drive." The Broncos kicked a field goal in overtime to win.

The Fumble

The very next year, the 1987 AFC championship involved the same two teams, playing in Denver. The Broncos were up 7 points with five minutes to play, and this time it was Browns quarterback Bernie Kosar who led his team on a long drive, one that might have lived on in NFL lore if not for what happened next. Running back Earnest Byner took a handoff at the 8-yard line, and he looked like he would score—but he

WORDS TO KNOW

OVERTIME RULES:
Overtime happens when a game is tied at the end of the fourth quarter. If the team that gets the ball first scores a touchdown, the game is over and they win. If they score a field goal, the other team gets a chance to tie it with a field goal of their own or win the game with a touchdown. If the game is still tied after both teams have had a turn on offense, the next score wins. Regular season games are called a tie if no one scores in ten minutes of overtime; playoff games go on until someone scores. (In high school and college, overtime means teams take turns trying to score from the same spot on the field.)

Perfect Play

Give yourself six points if you can match this touchdown to it's perfect shadow!

fumbled on the 1-yard line. Denver recovered the ball and held on to win the game. And the Cleveland Browns still have never been to a Super Bowl.

The Shove

Heading into the AFC title game after the 2022 season, Cincinnati quarterback Joe Burrow had never lost to the Chiefs; the team had in fact won the previous year's championship game at Arrowhead Stadium. During that game, Chiefs all-pro quarterback Patrick Mahomes could barely walk on his sprained ankle, yet the teams were tied with 17 seconds left as Mahomes faced 3rd down and 4 at the 47-yard line. It looked like the game would go to overtime. Mahomes hobbled toward the sideline, reached the football forward, and got the first down, still too far away for a field goal. But a Cincinnati player shoved Mahomes with two hands after he was out of bounds. That shove gave the Chiefs an extra 15 yards, setting up a Harrison Butker 45-yard field goal and, the next week, a Super Bowl victory.

The Biggest Event in America

The AFL-NFL championship game was named the "Super Bowl" by Chiefs owner Lamar Hunt. Super, indeed. After more than fifty years, Super Bowl Sunday is an unofficial national holiday. The game has become much more than just a league championship. Many Americans—at least one-third of the population—watch the game on television, while people throw parties and watch with their friends and families.

The last few Super Bowls have been watched by well over one hundred million people. The only sporting event in the world that is more significant is soccer's World Cup.

Roman Numerals

The NFL uses Roman numerals to number the Super Bowls except for Super Bowl 50. You may have learned about these in school. Roman numerals use letters to represent numbers: I means 1, V means 5, X means 10, and L means 50. It gets a bit more complicated—IV means 4, while VI means 6 because you subtract the smaller number if it comes first. The list in this chapter goes in order, so you can figure out for yourself how to count to 58 in Roman numerals.

Super Bowls are numbered starting with Super Bowl I after the 1966 season. This is because the regular season lasts from September through December, but the championship game isn't played until the next year. The Kansas City Chiefs won the Super Bowl in 2023, but they were the champions of the season that was played in the fall of 2022.

The 1960s–1980s: Your Grandparents' Super Bowls

Super Bowl I was quite a long time ago, back when your grandparents could only watch three or so television channels, and most families did not even have a color television. This was the era during which football became rapidly more popular each year. In the 1960s, the World Series was the most significant American sports championship. By the end of the 1980s, the World Series was still a big deal...but not as big as the Super Bowl.

Eureka!

Gold was discovered in California in 1848, and large numbers of gold diggers flocked to the West Coast starting in 1849. The new arrivals were nicknamed 49ers. Nearly one hundred years later, the All-America Football Conference created a franchise in San Francisco, and the team took on the 49ers name. Sourdough Sam, the 49ers mascot, is a cheerful football-loving gold digger.

I. **Packers 35, Chiefs 10.** This was the first AFL-NFL championship game, but it wasn't yet called the Super Bowl.
II. **Packers 33, Raiders 14.** Packers coach Vince Lombardi won his last NFL championship.
III. **Jets 16, (Baltimore) Colts 7.** Joe Namath's Jets showed everyone that the AFL was just as good as the NFL.
IV. **Chiefs 23, Vikings 7.** This was the first of four Vikings Super Bowl appearances; they haven't won yet.
V. **(Baltimore) Colts 16, Cowboys 13.** Chuck Howley of the Cowboys was voted the game's most valuable player, even though his team lost.
VI. **Cowboys 24, Dolphins 3.**
VII. **Dolphins 14, Washington 7.** The 1972 Dolphins became the first team in NFL history to complete an undefeated season.

VIII. **Dolphins 24, Vikings 7.** The Dolphins were the first team to appear in the Super Bowl three years in a row.

IX. **Steelers 16, Vikings 6.** This was the era of the Steel Curtain defense led by Mean Joe Greene.

X. **Steelers 21, Cowboys 17.** The Steelers came from behind with two touchdowns in the fourth quarter, then intercepted a pass on the last play of the game.

XI. **Raiders 32, Vikings 14.** Raiders head coach and future Hall of Famer John Madden won his only Super Bowl.

XII. **Cowboys 27, Broncos 10.**

XIII. **Steelers 35, Cowboys 31.** The Steelers won again in the matchup of the greatest teams of the 1970s.

XIV. **Steelers 31, Rams 19.** The Steelers won their fourth Super Bowl in four tries.

XV. **Raiders 27, Eagles 10.** This is the first Super Bowl that the author remembers watching—which is the first one your parents remember?

XVI. **49ers 26, Bengals 21.** San Francisco quarterback Joe Montana led his team to a 20-0 halftime lead.

XVII. **Washington 27, Dolphins 17.** Washington quarterback Joe Theismann won his only Super Bowl.

XVIII. **(Los Angeles) Raiders 38, Washington 9.** This would be the last victory for the AFC for fourteen years.

XIX. **49ers 38, Dolphins 16.** In his only Super Bowl appearance, Miami quarterback Dan Marino lost to Joe Montana's 49ers.

XX. **Bears 46, Patriots 10.** Coach Mike Ditka led his overwhelming favorite Bears to a convincing victory. In the lead-up to the game, the Bears recorded the famous "Super Bowl Shuffle" song and music video. Hall of Fame running back Walter Payton rapped: "Well, they call me Sweetness, and I like to dance…"

XXI. **Giants 39, Broncos 20.** Giants coach Bill Parcells won his first of three Super Bowl appearances.

Football GREAT

Joe Namath's Guarantee

Jets quarterback Joe Namath "guaranteed" that his team would win Super Bowl III, even though the Colts were heavily favored. Namath proved the media and the analysts wrong and earned the MVP award in the game. He was one of professional football's first superstars, appearing in movies and TV shows when he wasn't playing football.

XXII. **Washington 42, Broncos 10.** Washington quarterback Doug Williams not only became the first Black quarterback in the Super Bowl; he was also the game's MVP.

XXIII. **49ers 20, Bengals 16.** Joe Montana threw the winning TD to John Taylor with thirty-four seconds remaining, but 49ers receiver Jerry Rice was the MVP.

XXIV. **49ers 55, Broncos 10.** Ho-hum, Joe Montana won his fourth Super Bowl and his third MVP award.

The 1990s: Your Parents' Super Bowls

In 1990, the Super Bowl was a big television event, the biggest in the country. Even though cable television with dozens or hundreds of channels was available to most Americans, still, seventy-three million people watched, simply crushing the next-most-popular show (*America's Funniest Home Videos*). There were only 250 million people total in the United States then! By 2023, the Super Bowl had grown to 113 million viewers out of 330 million people in the USA. Try looking up the most-watched television broadcasts of all time. The moon landing of 1969 is first, then come pretty much nothing but Super Bowls.

MVP

Bart Starr of the Green Bay Packers was the most valuable player for the first two Super Bowls, and Joe Namath earned the honor in Super Bowl III. Starr and Namath also share the same alma mater, the University of Alabama. Tom Brady (the long-time Patriot who brought his winning ways with him when he moved to the Buccaneers in 2020) has won five Super Bowl MVP awards, the most ever of any NFL player.

XXV. **Giants 20, Bills 19.** Scott Norwood's 47-yard field goal attempt went wide right as time expired.

XXVI. **Washington 37, Bills 24.**

XXVII. **Cowboys 52, Bills 17.** Dallas quarterback Troy Aikman won his first of three Super Bowls.

XXVIII. **Cowboys 30, Bills 13.** The Bills tied the Vikings and the Broncos with four Super Bowl appearances and four losses.

XXIX. **49ers 49, Chargers 26.** This time, the 49ers were led by quarterback Steve Young, who threw six touchdowns.

XXX. **Cowboys 27, Steelers 17.**

Helmet Catch

With the Giants trailing in the fourth quarter of Super Bowl XLII, Eli Manning seemed like he was going to be sacked—and that the Patriots would win. But he evaded the rush and threw the ball far downfield, where receiver David Tyree was covered well by Rodney Harrison. Tyree jumped over Harrison, pinning the ball to his own helmet while being tackled. He maintained possession and completed the most improbable catch in Super Bowl history, setting up the Giants for their winning score. This was the very last catch Tyree ever made in an NFL game.

Left Shark

The 2015 halftime show featured pop singer Katy Perry. During her song "Teenage Dream," two dancers in 7-foot-tall shark costumes danced alongside Katy. However, the shark on the left seemed to have no rhythm at all! Left Shark's terrible dancing became a brief national sensation.

XXXI.   **Packers 35, Patriots 21.** QB Brett Favre led a resurgence of the Packers franchise, which had not seen such good times since the days of coach Vince Lombardi.

XXXII.   **Broncos 31, Packers 24.** Though the Broncos had lost four previous Super Bowls, they won this time behind a tremendous rushing attack.

XXXIII.   **Broncos 34, Falcons 19.** Quarterback John Elway won his second straight Super Bowl and the MVP trophy as well.

XXXIV.   **(St. Louis) Rams 23, Titans 16.** This year's Rams were the "Greatest Show on Turf." But the Titans had one last play from the 10-yard line. Mike Jones tackled receiver Kevin Dyson at the 1-yard line to seal the game.

The 2000s: The Rise of the Patriots

In the early 2000s, the Patriots became the second franchise to win three Super Bowls over the course of four years. Of course, they weren't the only winners in those years, as you'll see in the list here.

XXXV.   **Ravens 34, Giants 7.** The Ravens defense dominated this game, allowing only a special teams touchdown.

XXXVI.   **Patriots 20, (St. Louis) Rams 17.** Kicker Adam Vinatieri nailed a 48-yard field goal to end the game. First-year starting quarterback Tom Brady was MVP.

XXXVII.   **Buccaneers 48, Raiders 21.** The Tampa defense intercepted quarterback Rich Gannon five times, returning three for touchdowns.

XXXVIII.   **Patriots 32, Panthers 29.** Once again Adam Vinatieri won the game with a last-second field goal, and once again quarterback Tom Brady was the MVP.

XXXIX.   **Patriots 24, Eagles 21.** Vinatieri, Brady, and coach Bill Belichick won another close game.

Lost Player

What's going on? To find out, think of a word that best fits each of the clues. Write a word on the numbered line, then transfer each letter into the grid and the clues until you get the answer to the riddle.

Why did the football coach shake the vending machine?

1	2		3	4	5	6	7	8		9	10	11
12	13	14	15	16	17	18		19	20	21	22	!

Where you wear a glove

___ ___ ___ ___
9 20 5 8

Opposite of loud

___ ___ ___ ___ ___
12 13 10 2 6

Opposite of dry

___ ___ ___
3 7 16

Piece of equipment that stops a car

___ ___ ___ ___ ___
19 15 14 22 17

What happens when a car doesn't stop

___ ___ ___ ___ ___
21 18 4 11 1

Philly Special

In Super Bowl LII, the Eagles were up by 3 points over the Patriots nearing halftime. On fourth and goal, the Eagles chose not to kick a field goal. Instead, quarterback Nick Foles went into some odd motion; the ball was snapped not to the quarterback but to a running back, who pitched to tight end Trey Burton. Burton threw his first and only NFL pass into the end zone, where it was caught. . .by Nick Foles. As commemorated now in a statue outside the Eagles stadium, Foles went to his coach Doug Pederson right before fourth down and said, "You want Philly Philly?" Pederson told his quarterback, "Yeah, let's do it."

XL.   **Steelers 21, Seahawks 10.** Receiver Hines Ward and running back Jerome Bettis were the offensive heroes of the Steelers, who had just barely made the playoffs.

XLI.   **Colts 29, Bears 17.** Peyton Manning, who had been a top-rated quarterback for seven years without a championship, showed he could come through in a big game.

XLII.   **Giants 17, Patriots 14.** David Tyree's famous "helmet catch" helped defeat New England, who had not lost a game all year until the Super Bowl.

XLIII.   **Steelers 27, Cardinals 23.** The game ended with an amazing touchdown pass to MVP Santonio Holmes in the back corner of the end zone.

XLIV.   **Saints 31, Colts 17.** Saints quarterback and MVP Drew Brees led a come-from-behind victory against the favored Colts.

The 2010s: Your Older Cousins' Super Bowls

By the 2010s, fewer Americans were watching television, as streaming services gradually took hold. But the Super Bowl—and its halftime show—is a popular event for most of the country. The Super Bowl halftime shows in the twenty-first century became enormous, nationally televised live concerts. The list of performers reads like a popular music hall of fame. Shows in the 2010s included musicians popular in the 1960s (The Who), in the 1980s (Madonna), and today (Beyoncé). Even people who don't really like football often love the halftime show!

XLV.   **Packers 31, Steelers 25.**

XLVI.   **Giants 21, Patriots 17.** Eli Manning won the Super Bowl for the second time, one more (at the time!) than his brother Peyton.

XLVII. **Ravens 34, 49ers 31.** The 49ers, behind quarterback Colin Kaepernick, *almost* came back from way behind after a power outage at the Superdome that stopped the game for half an hour.

XLVIII. **Seahawks 43, Broncos 8.** The Seahawks scored a safety on the game's first play. Denver quarterback Peyton Manning never did figure out Seattle's smothering defense.

XLIX. **Patriots 28, Seahawks 24.** It looked like the Seahawks would win after a miracle catch by Jermaine Kearse. On the 1-yard line, Seattle tried to throw a pass for the winning TD, but Malcolm Butler's amazing interception sealed the game for New England.

50 (L). **Broncos 24, Panthers 10.** Peyton Manning won his final Super Bowl.

LI. **Patriots 34, Falcons 28.** The Falcons were leading 28-3 in the third quarter, but Tom Brady brought the Patriots back. New England drove 91 yards to force overtime, where James White ran for a game-winning touchdown. This was both the largest comeback win in Super Bowl history *and* the first overtime game.

LII. **Eagles 41, Patriots 33.** The Eagles' backup quarterback Nick Foles led an upset of the mighty Patriots and regular season MVP Tom Brady.

LIII. **Patriots 13, Rams 3.** Tom Brady won his sixth Super Bowl, the one many people at the time thought would be his last.

The 2020s: Super Bowls You Might Remember

The 2020s marked the crowning end of Tom Brady's career, as well as the rise of the Chiefs and Patrick Mahomes. Though they didn't win *every* Super Bowl you can remember, the Chiefs have been the team to beat for many of the years you've been watching the NFL.

Football GREAT

Colin Kaepernick

Colin Kaepernick was a leading NFL quarterback for the San Francisco 49ers. He had three chances to complete an epic comeback against the Ravens in Super Bowl XLVII, but the Ravens defense managed to bat away three pass attempts from the 2-yard line. He was that close to being an NFL champion.

Three years later, after consulting with a US marine, Kaepernick began taking a knee during the national anthem as a way of bringing attention to the large number of Black people who have been shot by police officers without consequences. After he became as well known for his political activism as for his football prowess, no NFL team would hire him. Eventually, the NFL paid Kaepernick to settle charges that the league leaders had illegally worked together to keep him out of the league. Since then, he has continued work as an activist, donating and raising money for a variety of causes. In 2020, NFL commissioner Roger Goodell stated, "I wish we had listened earlier, Kaep, to what you were kneeling about, and what you were trying to bring attention to."

Football Fill In

Get ready to pass, punt, and run! If you're a rookie player, you can choose from the answer words scattered around the puzzle on the next page. Pro ball players should be able to complete the puzzle without looking!

ACROSS

2. A six-point score earned when the ball crosses the goal line

6. Player who receives the snap during a field goal attempt

9. Fake grass sometimes used in football stadiums

11. Area created by the offensive line to protect the quarterback

13. Offensive players who catch passes

14. A person or animal that represents a team

15. To throw the ball

17. A football field has 100 of these

18. Person who makes sure the teams follow the rules

21. Three points earned when the ball is kicked through the goalpost

24. Arena where football games are played

25. People who cheer for a team

26. Offensive player who throws passes

DOWN

1. Person on the sideline who guides the team through plays

3. A group of players who gather together to discuss the next play

4. What the referee blows to stop a play

5. Offensive player who snaps the ball

7. Players who control the ball and try to score

8. What the fans eat in the stands

10. A group of football players who work together

12. One way to stop a player from running

16. What a player wears to protect his head

19. Game played where the school's graduates come to watch

20. A defensive player who tries to keep receivers from catching passes

21. What a referee throws to indicate a foul

22. Players who keep the other team from scoring

23. When more than four defensive players rush the quarterback

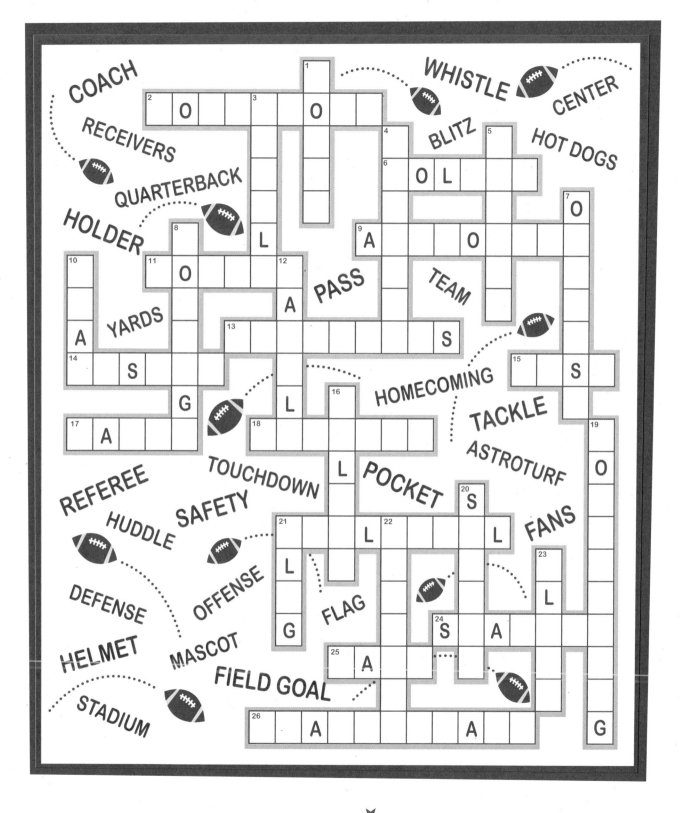

Home Field Advantage in the Super Bowl?

The site for each Super Bowl is chosen by a committee, years ahead of the game. In 2016, the NFL selected the city of Tampa and the stadium where the Buccaneers play as the host of Super Bowl LV. The Buccaneers became the first true home team ever in the Super Bowl—it was the first time that the game was played in the home stadium of one of the participating teams!

LIV. **Chiefs 31, 49ers 20.** This was a battle between up-and-coming quarterbacks. Patrick Mahomes of the Chiefs was in his third year, but he had already won an NFL MVP award. Jimmy Garoppolo had been the backup to Tom Brady for four years, but he got his chance to be a starting quarterback in 2019 with the 49ers. The 49ers led by 10 points in the fourth quarter, but game MVP Mahomes led three straight touchdown drives to make the final score seem like a Chiefs blowout.

LV. **Buccaneers 31, Chiefs 9.** During the COVID-19 pandemic, there were times when it didn't seem likely that the Super Bowl would ever happen! The greatest young quarterback and defending champion—Patrick Mahomes—faced the six-time champion widely considered to be the Greatest of All Time—Tom Brady. Brady had moved from the Patriots to the Buccaneers in the off-season. The game itself was lopsided, in large part because the Chiefs' offensive line injuries meant that Mahomes hardly ever had time to throw downfield. Brady threw three touchdowns and was named MVP. Again. But for the final time.

LVI. **Rams 23, Bengals 20.** The Bengals hadn't been to a Super Bowl since the 1988 season and had not won a playoff game in thirty years. But shouts of "Who Dey?"—the Bengals signature cheer—returned as quarterback Joe Burrow led Cincinnati to a lead just after halftime. But Rams receiver and MVP Cooper Kupp caught his second touchdown pass to put the Rams ahead for good. Defensive lineman Aaron Donald, who had terrorized the Bengals all game, tackled Burrow on the final play, causing the final pass to fall incomplete.

LVII. **Chiefs 38, Eagles 35.** The Chiefs were in the Super Bowl *again* under head coach Andy Reid, this time against the team that had fired Reid a decade earlier. Chiefs tight end Travis Kelce faced Eagles center Jason Kelce—his brother. Both teams had 14-3 records entering the Super Bowl. So even beforehand, it seemed like the game would be close and exciting. And sure enough, Patrick Mahomes faced 3rd and long near the end of a tied game. His pass was incomplete…but the Eagles were called for defensive holding. The penalty allowed the Chiefs to run down the clock and kick the game-winning field goal.

LVIII. **Chiefs 25, 49ers 22.** In the second quarter, the 49ers led the Chiefs by 10 points—just like four years earlier. Defense and turnovers dominated the game until late in the second half when the 49ers muffed a punt at the 16-yard line. Patrick Mahomes threw a touchdown pass on the next play. The 49ers answered with a touchdown, but they missed the extra point. So the Chiefs kicked a field goal to send the game into overtime. There, Mahomes took over the Chiefs offense on the 25-yard line knowing that they had to score, or they'd lose. Of course, MVP Mahomes led a 13-play drive and threw the winning touchdown to Mecole Hardman from the 3-yard line.

CHAPTER 4

College Football

FUN FACT

NCAA

Football and other sports are an important part of college life. NCAA stands for the National Collegiate Athletic Association. The NCAA was founded in 1906 primarily to govern football, but now this organization runs all sports played by its member schools.

Football GREAT

Emmitt Smith

Running back Emmitt Smith is best known for his thirteen years with the Dallas Cowboys when he helped lead the team to three Super Bowl victories. Because Emmitt was so successful in the pros, many fans forget his outstanding career at the University of Florida, which earned him a place in the College Football Hall of Fame. After he began playing in the NFL, he continued to take classes. In 1996, he graduated with a degree in public recreation.

What Is the NCAA?

The National Collegiate Athletic Association (NCAA) is the governing body for just about all college football. Member schools join one of three divisions:

- **Division III** schools are usually small and do not formally offer athletic scholarships. In Division III, athletics are viewed as merely extracurricular activities, not as a way for the school to make money.
- **Division II** schools offer athletic scholarships, though they have a limited number to offer. These programs generally do not have the enormous money or fan support necessary to participate in Division I, but the teams are competitive.
- **Division I** is the highest level of NCAA football. Teams have large stadiums, and many fans come to watch every game. They offer large numbers of athletic scholarships. The schools make lots and lots of money from selling tickets, merchandise, and television rights, though the schools are forbidden from paying their players any money.

Division I has two subdivisions:

- **The Championship Subdivision** used to be called Division I-AA. These are the smaller schools, which attract fewer than fifteen thousand fans on average to their games. At the end of the year, sixteen teams enter a playoff to determine a champion.
- **The Football Bowl Subdivision** used to be called Division I-A. These are the football powers that want to contend for a national championship. Virtually all of the teams you see on TV are from this subdivision.

For many years, the Football Bowl Subdivision had no playoff, and the champion was voted on by reporters. Starting in 1998, a playoff determined the national champion. As of 2024, twelve teams have been chosen for the playoffs.

College Football Compared to NFL Football

You might not notice the different kinds of players, the different schedules, or the different rules of college football. Here's a quick summary.

Who Plays?

The most important difference is also the most obvious: College football players are actual college students who live on campus, go to class, and can graduate from the school after several years. They still participate in college life in many of the same ways that physics majors do, and some of them may even be physics majors. The NCAA forbids teams from paying players directly, though some of them are given a full scholarship. And players can earn "NIL" money by endorsing products.

A college football player is only allowed to play for their team for four years while they are a student. Since it takes most students a while to develop their skills and their bodies to the necessary level, most players are starters for only one or two years. Fans get used to watching new players each year.

A Shorter Schedule

The college schedule is shorter than the NFL schedule. Play starts in late August when most of the really good teams play weaker teams in order to start the season with some wins. Conference play usually begins in late September. After twelve games, the regular season schedule is complete by

ATHLETIC SCHOLARSHIP: Both the NFL and some colleges make millions every year from their teams. However, colleges are not allowed to pay their players directly. Instead, players are often offered athletic scholarships where all of the player's college fees and living expenses are paid for him.

NIL: In 2021, the NCAA lost a court case and had to change its rules about players earning money. Since then, any college athlete is allowed to make money using their "Name, Image, or Likeness," or NIL. That means that since many college players are quite famous, they may accept money to appear in advertisements. Colleges are still not allowed to pay their players directly, but players can benefit from making their own NIL deals.

REDSHIRT: Often, a first-year college student isn't ready to play regularly for his team, or a player might get hurt right before the season. If the team agrees to keep him out of most games, then the year becomes a redshirt year, meaning it doesn't count toward the player's four years of eligibility.

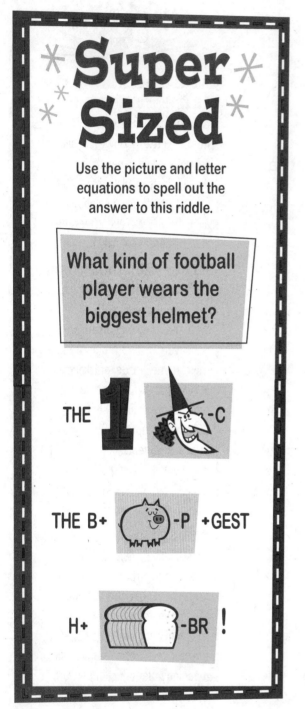

Super Sized

Use the picture and letter equations to spell out the answer to this riddle.

What kind of football player wears the biggest helmet?

THE **1** [witch] -C

THE B+ [pig] -P +GEST

H+ [bread loaf] -BR !

late November. Football Bowl Subdivision teams that win at least five games can be invited to play in bowl games, which happen in late December or early January. The very best teams play in their conference championship games in early December and can be chosen to play in the College Football Playoff.

Different Rules

College football is just about the same game that the NFL plays. There are a few minor differences that you'll only notice if you watch carefully. For example, college teams get the ball on the 3-yard line to try for an extra point; NFL teams get the ball on the 2-yard line. The hash marks, where the ball is put in play, are farther apart in college. The NFL requires a receiver to get both feet in bounds to catch the ball fairly; college receivers only need one foot down. Both levels play for four fifteen-minute quarters, but they have different rules about when the clock stops and when it runs. As a result, college games usually take longer to play than pro games.

Perhaps the biggest difference between pro and college football is the overtime procedure. In the NFL, overtime is played just like the rest of the game, but a touchdown wins the game and the other team doesn't get to try. In college, one team gets the ball at the other team's 25-yard line and tries to score. Then, the other team gets the ball at the same spot. Whoever scores more points wins. If the teams are still tied, they go again until one team comes out of overtime with more points than the other.

The Fans

NFL teams represent a city. People become fans if they grew up near the team. The NCAA teams represent their school as well as their community. Most of the student body has some connection to the football team. Some students are band members or cheerleaders, and student managers help the coaches run drills. Students who aren't directly involved with the team might at least know someone on campus who is involved—maybe they're in a class with the star quarterback or they use the fitness center at the same time as the cheerleading squad. Students usually get cheap tickets and dress in school colors ready to make noise in the crowd.

Because football is such an important part of their social life during college, people who go to colleges with football teams tend to develop a lifelong love for their team. Colleges have alumni clubs, in which graduates pay money to get special seating at games, meetings with coaches, and parties at the stadium with their friends. Graduates bring their children to games, building loyalty throughout families.

But not all fans are students and alumni. A college team draws fans from the surrounding community. Especially when there's no NFL team nearby, college football becomes the biggest event on Saturdays and throughout the year. For example, most of the state of Nebraska is a long day's drive from Denver, where the closest NFL team plays. But they're not concerned. To them, it is the University of Nebraska Cornhuskers games on Saturdays that they care most about. Los Angeles, California, didn't have a team for a while after the Rams and Raiders left in 1995. So the two biggest college teams, the UCLA Bruins and the USC Trojans, became the true hometown favorites.

Football GREAT

Joe Burrow and Ja'Marr Chase

QB Joe Burrow and wide receiver Ja'Marr Chase played two years together at Louisiana State University (LSU). When Burrow was a senior and Chase was a sophomore, the LSU Tigers won the college football national championship. Chase caught twenty of Burrow's sixty touchdown passes that year and almost a third of Burrow's most-in-the-country 5,671 passing yards. Both players were drafted by the Cincinnati Bengals, and they continued their winning ways with playoff and Super Bowl appearances.

Conferences for Other Sports

Most teams play in the same conference for all sports, not just football. For example, in the 2006 football season, the University of Alabama won the Southeastern Conference (SEC). In the spring of that same school year, Alabama won the SEC softball regular season title.

INDEPENDENTS: An independent team is not part of a conference. Only three Football Bowl Subdivision teams are independent: Notre Dame, the University of Massachusetts, and the University of Connecticut. And even Notre Dame plays a half schedule in the ACC.

How College Football Is Organized: Conferences

More than one hundred teams make up the Football Bowl Subdivision of NCAA Division I. Teams play only twelve regular season games each year, so there's no way that a team can play every other team. A conference consists of a dozen or more teams who agree to play a set schedule among the conference teams each year. Years ago, a conference contained teams from only one region of the country—that's why it's called the Atlantic Coast Conference, for example.

Conferences have rules to ensure that every team makes some money each year. For example, if a team plays in a bowl game, some of the money they make is distributed among all the teams in the conference. This way, a team makes money even in years when it isn't doing well. Another reason for being part of a conference is the schedule. Since about eight of every year's games are conference games, the school only has to look for three or four other games to schedule. Of those eight or so conference games, usually four are guaranteed to be home games. Without a conference, it might be difficult to find teams to play, especially teams that are willing to play as a visiting team.

NCAA Football Bowl Subdivision Conferences

The five best-known and most important conferences are called the Power Five. These conferences include most of the schools that might challenge for a national championship:

- **The Southeastern Conference (SEC):** Schools in this conference come from as far north as Kentucky and as far west as Texas. The most recent expansion in 2024 brought the league up to sixteen teams with the addition of the University of Texas and the University of Oklahoma. In recent years, Alabama, the University of Georgia, and Louisiana State have made it to the national championship game. In fact, only two championship games since the playoff system began have *not* included an SEC team!

- **The Big Ten:** You might think that a conference called the Big Ten would include ten teams, but it currently has eighteen schools. The Big Ten had only ten teams from 1950 until 1990 when they added Penn State. Originally, the teams were from the Midwest, but today they include both Rutgers (in New Jersey) and Washington (in Seattle). Every Big Ten title game since 2017 has been won by either Ohio State or Michigan.

- **The Atlantic Coast Conference (ACC):** In the ACC, the great basketball programs from the University of North Carolina, Duke University, Wake Forest University, North Carolina State University, and the rest of the conference have often taken the spotlight away from football. In the 1990s and 2000s, the conference added several "football schools," including the University of Miami, Florida State University, and Boston College. Now the ACC has seventeen teams, not all of which are located near the Atlantic coast. Also, Notre Dame plays a partial schedule against ACC teams. All but one of the ACC title games since 2011 have been won by Clemson or Florida State.

- **The Big 12:** Way back in the 1900s, eight colleges from the Great Plains formed the Big 8 conference, which added four schools to become the Big 12 in 1994. In the 2010s and 2020s, most of the original Big 12 football schools left the conference. Since then, the conference has expanded to sixteen schools from all over the country. Fifteen of twenty-two Big 12 title games were won by the University of Oklahoma or the University of Texas; however, these schools are now in the SEC.

Co-Champions

Before 1998, the national champion was determined exclusively by a vote of football reporters and coaches. If the reporters and coaches chose different teams, as they did in 1997, both teams were recognized as national champions. From 1998 to 2014, the winner of a two-team playoff called the Bowl Championship Series (BCS) was recognized by the NCAA as the national champion. Occasionally, however, the final reporters' poll of the year ranked a different team number one. In that case, the national championship was shared by the BCS winner and the number one team in the reporters' poll. This happened in 2003: Louisiana State University won the BCS championship, but the reporters voted the University of Southern California as the best team. Both teams are considered to be 2003 national champions.

The Biggest Mascot

At the beginning of every half, the Big 12 Colorado Buffaloes are led onto the football field by Ralphie, a live buffalo.

The Cutest Mascot

The mascot of the Northern Illinois Huskies is a real, live Siberian Husky dog named Mission. He is trained to give cheerleaders high-fives when Northern Illinois scores.

- **The Pac-12:** In 1915, four West Coast schools formed the Pacific Coast Conference: University of California, Berkeley; University of Washington; University of Oregon; and Oregon Agricultural College (now Oregon State University). By 1978, the conference changed its name to the Pac-10 and added more schools from Washington, California, and Arizona. In 2011, Utah and Colorado joined, making it the Pac-12. The University of Southern California has won thirty-seven conference titles, more than twice as many as any other team.

These five conferences usually have the best players and the most television and fan attention. Some of the conferences even have their own TV networks! The other Football Bowl Subdivision conferences have strong programs that are competitive with each other, but they usually have a hard time when facing power conference teams. In fact, a bigger program will often pay a smaller team a lot of money to play a game at the bigger school's home field. Why? The big team gets a home game that they're likely to win. The smaller team may not like the idea of getting crushed in a road game, but the money they make might pay for a large number of scholarships or a new fitness center. And who knows? A few times every year, a school from a non–power conference beats a big-time team. In 2019, for example, the mighty Georgia Tech Yellow Jackets of the ACC lost to the Citadel Bulldogs of the Southern Conference.

Determining a National Champion

A twelve-team tournament determines the national champion. A selection committee made up of thirteen members evaluates and ranks the top twenty-five teams. They begin publishing their rankings in October, though those midseason rankings are meaningless. After the conference championship games, the teams are re-ranked, and then the top six conference champions plus the next six highest-ranked teams make the playoff. The four highest-ranked teams get byes into the second round.

The first-round games are played at the home field of the higher-ranked team. The quarterfinals are played on New Year's Day or New Year's Eve as part of the traditional bowl games; the semifinals are played the following week at the sites of bowl games. Then, in mid-January, the semifinal winners play a national championship in a major national event.

National Champions	
2006	Florida Gators
2007	Louisiana State Tigers
2008	Florida Gators
2009	Alabama Crimson Tide
2010	Auburn Tigers
2011	Alabama Crimson Tide
2012	Alabama Crimson Tide
2013	Florida State Seminoles
2014	Ohio State Buckeyes
2015	Alabama Crimson Tide
2016	Clemson Tigers
2017	Alabama Crimson Tide
2018	Clemson Tigers
2019	Louisiana State Tigers
2020	Alabama Crimson Tide
2021	Georgia
2022	Georgia
2023	Michigan

Eddie Robinson

In 1941, Grambling State University, a Division I-AA college in northern Louisiana, hired coach Eddie Robinson. Until 1997 (that's fifty-six years!), Robinson coached the Tigers to 408 victories, the second most ever for a coach in Division I. More than two hundred of his players entered the NFL. That would be a lot for a huge Division I program, let alone for a coach in a lower division.

FUN FACT

Cold, Blue Turf?

Bowl games are usually played in warm places like Hawaii, Florida, or California. But the Famous Idaho Potato Bowl is played in the very cold city of Boise, Idaho. The field for this bowl game is artificial turf, not natural grass—and the turf is painted blue! Rumor has it that migrating geese sometimes crash into the blue turf because they think it's a lake!

Rivalry Story: The "Kick Six"

In 2013, Auburn and Alabama were tied with only one second remaining. Alabama tried to kick a very long field goal for the win. Auburn's Chris Davis waited in the back of the end zone just in case the field goal came up short, which it did, falling into Davis's hands. Davis returned the missed field goal into the field of play and then up the sideline, where he broke free. Auburn radio announcer Rod Bramblett joyously called out, "Davis is gonna run it all the way back! Auburn is gonna win the football game! Auburn is gonna win the football game!"

Bowl Games

Even though only four teams make the College Football Play-off, most teams get to play in a postseason game called a bowl game. What are these, and why are there so many?

The Way It Was

Before the 1990s, there weren't very many bowl games, and each one was extra special and extra popular. In those days, most people couldn't see more than one or two college football games per week. If you lived, say, in Ohio, you might never have seen a Pac-12 game all year. The bowl games were the fans' opportunity to see some of the great teams they had heard so much about. As for the teams, only the winner of a conference or a few selected other great teams got to play in a bowl. The six New Year's Day bowl games—the Rose Bowl, Cotton Bowl, Orange Bowl, Sugar Bowl, Fiesta Bowl, and Peach Bowl—were the highlight of the season for the fans.

Bowl Games Today

After the 2023 season, there were forty-three bowl games played in the weeks before and the week after New Year's Day. More than half of the Football Bowl Subdivision teams play in a bowl; virtually all Power Five conference teams play in a bowl. Now that most regular season games are on television throughout the country and almost any team can make it to a bowl, they are not as big a deal as they used to be. In fact, there are so many bowl games that even teams with losing records are sometimes invited to play.

But they're still fun! Millions of fans watch the games and the players have a good time. Teams that make it to bowls are allowed extra practice time to prepare. Teams make use of this time not only to get ready for the bowl but also to give younger players experience so they'll be ready to replace the graduating seniors the next year. Most bowls may not be truly special games, but they'll keep being played as long as people keep watching.

The Best College Football Rivalries

Most schools have a single most-hated rival, a team they play only once each year but whose game dominates the season. A true rivalry means that, during the first part of the season, fans of both teams actively root against their rival, no matter who they play. Some fans would rather go 1-10 while beating their rival than go 10-1 with a loss to their rival. Most rivalry games are played the week before Thanksgiving, though some are played on Thanksgiving weekend.

Here is a look at the four best-known college football rivalries:

Auburn-Alabama

The Iron Bowl matches the two biggest football schools in the state of Alabama. The teams didn't play each other between 1907 and 1947 because the schools couldn't agree on how to get unbiased referees. The Alabama Crimson Tide have won more games than the Auburn Tigers in the history of the rivalry.

Stanford-California

The Big Game, as it's known, pits these San Francisco Bay Area schools against each other every year. Both schools are best known for their strong academic programs, and they have produced plenty of NFL players. In the days leading up to the game, the California freshmen chemistry classes all get together for a special demonstration in which the professor turns a red flask blue with just one drop of a chemical. (Red is Stanford's color; blue and gold are California's colors.)

Rivalry Story: The Band Is on the Field!

One of the most famous plays occurred at the end of the 1982 Big Game between Stanford and California. Stanford QB John Elway led his team on a drive to take the lead with four seconds left. But on the kickoff, the Cal team made five backward passes and evaded all of the tacklers. The Stanford band, thinking the game was over, marched onto the field. California's Kevin Moen ran among the band and entered the end zone, where he knocked over a trombone player. Cal won 25-20.

The Stanford Axe

At a Cal-Stanford baseball game in 1899, Cal students stole an axe from the Stanford cheerleaders. Cal kept that axe in a bank vault for thirty-one years, until a crew of Stanford students launched an elaborate and successful plot to steal it back. Now, whichever team wins the Big Game gets to keep the axe for a year. At Stanford pep rallies, cheerleaders still refer to "the Stanford axe that California has wrongly stolen from us, that it is our responsibility to retrieve."

Rivalry Story

Legendary Ohio State coach Woody Hayes hated Michigan—not just the university but the whole state and anything associated with it. It is said that when the Ohio State team bus was running out of gas on the way home to Ohio, Coach Hayes refused to stop at any gas station in the state of Michigan, even if he might have to walk for miles to get more gas.

Ohio State-Michigan

These schools have won twenty national championships between the two of them, and together they have won nearly half of all Big Ten championships in conference history. As a result, the yearly Michigan-Ohio State game often decides the Big Ten champion. There is nothing more important to fans of these schools than beating their rival. Former OSU coach John Cooper won more than 70 percent of his games and three conference championships. But his record against Michigan was 2-10-1, so he was fired in 2000. Since then, Ohio State has won all but six games in this rivalry.

Army-Navy

Each branch of the United States armed forces has its own academy. To attend, a student must meet very strict academic and physical requirements. Everyone at the service academies, not just the athletes, gets a full scholarship. All students take challenging courses and receive military training, and they must spend several years in the armed forces when they graduate. Student life is quite different at Army and Navy (and Air Force) than it is at other Division I schools.

It's understandable, then, that the academies aren't usually in the hunt for a national championship. Yet the Army-Navy rivalry is perhaps the most intense in the country. Cadets and midshipmen arrive at the game in full uniform. They put on displays of push-ups when their team scores. The game is carried on the Armed Forces Network, meaning that everyone in the Army and the Navy, even people who are deployed overseas, can watch the game on television or listen to it over the radio. The game has always been an important television event in the United States. In fact, the first time that a replay was ever shown during a televised football game was during an Army-Navy game.

Go Team!

A very visible part of any football team are the cheerleaders! The first organized cheer was during a college football game over one hundred years ago, in 1898. Believe it or not, that original cheer is still being used at the University of Minnesota today! Use the decoder to fill in the blanks, and then give this cheer a try — outside of the house, of course!

A = ※
H = ★
I = ☆
N = ☆
O = ❀
S = ✳
Y = ☀

R※★, R※★, R※★!

✳K☆-U-M※★,

★❀❀-R※★!

★❀❀-R※★!

V※R✳☆T❀!

V※R✳☆T❀!

V※R✳☆T❀,

M☆☆☆-E-✳❀-T※★!

What's in a Name?

All college teams have some kind of nickname. Frequently, animals are used for both the nickname and the team mascot. Break the Letter Switch code (B=A, C=B, D=C, etc.) for the first row of names to learn the four most popular animal nicknames.

Some teams choose more unusual nicknames. Break the Vowel Switch code (A=I, E=O, I=U, O=A, U=E) for the second row of words to learn some of these lesser-known mascots!

The most popular mascots are:
FBHMFT   CVMMEPHT   UJHFST   MJPOT

Some more unusual mascots are:
PUNGIANS   KONGOREES   EWLS   BLIUHUNS

College Football Beyond Division I

Every year, thousands and thousands of good high school football players graduate and go to college. Only the very best are offered scholarships for Division I teams. Though the majority of these high school graduates will never make it to the NFL, they might not be ready to end their football careers. One option for them is to play football at a Division II or a Division III school.

Lower-division colleges don't have 100,000-seat stadiums and national television cameras at the games. At the same time, their games are usually much bigger events than high school games, with large stadiums, crowds, and a high quality of play. Fans of lower-division football teams point out that going to their games can be a better experience than going to a big school's games because admission is cheaper, the stadium is less cramped, and there's no need to fight for a parking space.

Perhaps the most fun aspect of Division II and III football is the national championship playoff at the end of the season. The very best teams get to host as many as three playoff games at home. The final in each division is shown on national television.

In Division III, the championship game is called the Amos Alonzo Stagg Bowl, named after the famous coach of the University of Chicago's football team from the early 1900s. The University of Mount Union, in Alliance, Ohio, has won thirteen Stagg Bowls—by far the most of any team.

Bill the Goat

Bill is the Naval Academy mascot. He's a live goat who attends every Army-Navy game. He has been kidnapped several times in history by cadets at both Air Force and Army, but each time Naval Intelligence tracked him down and obtained his release.

The Commander-in-Chief's Trophy

This coveted award is presented to the team with the best record in the yearly games between Army, Navy, and Air Force. Though Air Force has won the trophy the most times, Army has won it five times since 2017.

CHAPTER 5 High School Football

There's a Team for Everyone

The pros take center stage on Sundays, and college football seems to dominate fall Saturdays in America. But Friday nights belong to the high schools. Most high schools sponsor a football team. Since most teenagers attend high schools within their local area, high school teams truly represent communities. You have probably met some of the players on the nearby high school team, and you might even have relatives on a team. Maybe you'd like to play high school football one day.

Varsity, Junior Varsity, and Freshman Teams

The team that represents the school on Friday night includes the best players in the school, and it is called the varsity team. The majority of varsity players are juniors and seniors. Unless younger players are unusually fast or way bigger than normal for their age, they're probably not ready to play varsity.

Depending on the size of the school, there might be other teams to join. The junior varsity (JV) team often includes players who are not quite good enough to play regularly on the varsity, or perhaps players who are good enough to play varsity but who are still too young or too small to start. The JV team might play on Monday instead of Friday or might play a Friday afternoon game right before the varsity game. If the school is big enough, it might sponsor a third team, one just for freshmen. The lower-level teams give you a good way to play the game, have fun, and develop your skills. The best way to become good enough for the varsity team is to play hard and to play well at the freshman and JV levels.

Twin
Teammates

There are ten differences between uniforms and equipment shown here. Can you find them?

Did You Know?

Some players who carry the ball wear very tight pants. This makes it harder for the other team to grab their pants to stop them!

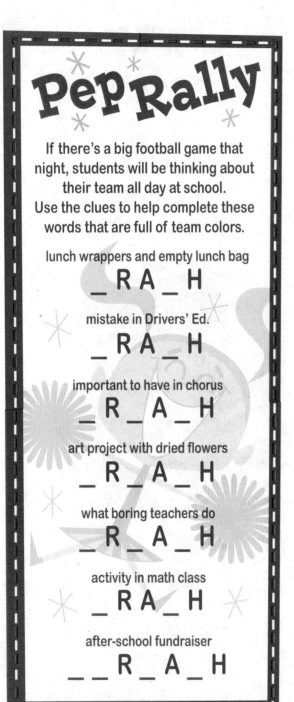

Pep Rally

If there's a big football game that night, students will be thinking about their team all day at school.
Use the clues to help complete these words that are full of team colors.

lunch wrappers and empty lunch bag

_ R A _ H

mistake in Drivers' Ed.

_ R A _ H

important to have in chorus

_ R _ A _ H

art project with dried flowers

_ R _ A _ H

what boring teachers do

_ R _ A _ H

activity in math class

_ R A _ H

after-school fundraiser

_ _ R _ A _ H

The Off-Season—Getting in Shape

The game of football requires enormous physical effort, and it can give your body a bit of a beating. You must be in good shape to play any kind of football, and the higher the level of your game, the more speed, strength, endurance, and flexibility you must develop. A high school football player cannot spend all summer just lying on the beach and playing video games. Someone who does so will likely not make it through the first practice, let alone any games.

A high school coach will usually give the players a summer workout program that will gradually build up the players' fitness. The idea is to come into pre-season practices ready to play hard. Off-season workouts include lots of running and weightlifting. The team might come in all together a couple of times per week for their workouts. Players who go on long vacations or who do special summer trips can still run, do push-ups and sit-ups, and find a place to do weightlifting occasionally.

Skill Camps

The summer is the time when many colleges offer camps to help players develop their skills. These may last a couple of days or as long as a week. The college's coaching staff often runs these camps. They show the players drills, films, and conditioning exercises that will help them develop into better players. The camps can be a chance to compete against and practice with top players from other schools. By the end of the camp, all players have a pretty good idea of what they can do well, which skills still need improvement, and who the really, really good players are.

A great way for a team to improve together over the summer is to play in a 7-on-7 league or to attend a 7-on-7 camp. Sure, it's important to develop individual skills, but it's even more crucial to play with your teammates in competitive situations. In a 7-on-7 game, quarterbacks can practice reading coverages and can learn how their receivers will react to different defenses. Defensive backs can practice not just one-on-one defense; they can also be part of an entire coverage scheme. If you're playing a game, then what you're doing feels like more than just practice. A great play can actually score a touchdown, just as in a real football game, and a mistake may cost points. The team is practicing under nearly real game conditions. When the team is faced with a truly real game in the fall, they will know how to react. They will have confidence in their teammates and in themselves, hopefully leading to a few extra wins.

Right Before the Season

The team gets together for two weeks or so of preseason practice. The coaching staff usually has two goals for this time:

- Teach the team how plays are called and what to do on each play.
- Improve players' techniques so everyone becomes a better player at their position.

To accomplish these goals, many different teaching tools might be used. For example, the team might have classroom meetings with a chalkboard and notebooks to explain how some plays are supposed to work. On another day, the team might watch video of a college team executing these plays successfully. Sometimes it's useful to watch video of yesterday's practice to show who ran the plays correctly or incorrectly.

What Is 7-on-7?

In a 7-on-7 drill, the offensive and defensive lines are removed so the team can focus just on the passing game. The defense plays with three linebackers and four defensive backs; the offense gets a center, five running backs or receivers, and a quarterback.

The Tip Drill

One of the defenders' favorite drills is called the tip drill. In one version, the coach throws a pass to a running receiver, who deliberately misses the catch and tips the ball in the air. The defenders have to catch the ball for an interception. If they can't catch the ball cleanly, they're taught to try to keep the ball in the air. Defenses love interceptions, and they can make an interception on every play of this drill.

Football GREAT

Reggie White

Reggie, a defensive end nicknamed the Minister of Defense, lived all of his early life in Chattanooga, Tennessee. He went to the Howard School of Academics and Technology for high school and the University of Tennessee for college. His NFL career included dominant years with both the Philadelphia Eagles and the Green Bay Packers.

On the field, a chunk of practice is devoted to skill development with the position coaches. During this time, the players run drills that help them practice a technique. For example, quarterbacks may work on hitting a target or on reading the safeties and throwing away from them. Linebackers may repeatedly practice taking a read step and dropping into coverage.

Another big chunk of preseason practice time is devoted to rehearsing plays. The offense might start by running the plays "on air," meaning that they just go through what they're supposed to do without any defense around. Next, a few managers or second-string players might hold pads and stand where defenders might be. Eventually, the offense knows the plays well enough to run them against a live defense.

Scouting the Opponent

Once the season starts, both the offense and the defense usually know all of the team's plays. The question then becomes which of these plays will work best against the next opponent. Figuring out which plays to use is called scouting, and it is one of the coaching staff's biggest jobs.

Well before each game, teams trade video. They send video of their old games to their next opponent. Before a game, the coaching staff watches this video carefully. They figure out who the opponent's best players are and which are the best units. They'll also try to find weak spots. Maybe their cornerbacks look really good, but their defensive linemen seem to get pushed back on every play. Then they decide what strategy to use to beat this team. They might need to use a power running game, mixed with a few deep passes if the safeties come up to stop the run. Whatever they decide, the coaches must have a clear plan ready before Monday's practice. That's when they start preparing the team for the game.

The Week Before a Game

Practice during the season runs a bit differently from pre-season practices. Much less time is set aside to work on skills and techniques because more time is necessary to establish and practice the week's game plan.

The Scout Team

Most football teams include a good number of players who don't get much playing time in games. These folks aren't the starters, and sometimes they aren't even the backups for the starters. But they can play an essential role in practice.

Once the coaching staff has scouted the upcoming opponent, they know how that opponent plays: what formations they use on offense, which kinds of plays they run, and what strategies they use on defense. To prepare for this opponent, the coaching staff chooses a scout team made up of nonstarters. The scout team pretends to be the upcoming opponent. Their job is to give the starters practice seeing the same kind of football team that they will see on Friday night. If enough players are available, two scout teams could be formed—one for offense, one for defense.

Early in the week, the coaches explain the game plan and practice the specific plays or defenses that will be used. First the offense and defense practice separately, making sure they know what to do. Toward the end of practice, the offense and defense will run against the scout team. The coaching staff can tell which of their ideas will work (and which won't) by noticing how the scout team does. If the scout team is stopping the offense, then the offense probably needs a new game plan.

By the end of the week, the players all know what to do. Practice might then consist of special game situations, like trying to score from the 2-yard line or stopping the offense on third down and long. Maybe the team will even play a ghost

Impersonating Star Players

If the next opponent has a really good player, the scout team might assign their best athlete to pretend to be that star. On some teams, the star player on the scout team gets to wear a special jersey with the number of the opposing player. Being chosen to impersonate the opponent's best player is a big deal for a scout team player.

HOMECOMING: One home game each fall is the homecoming game. That's when students who already graduated come back to the school to see each other and show their support for their former high school. Homecoming events include more than just a football game—usually there's also a parade, a dance, and maybe even other events.

Boarding School Football

There are options for high school beyond local public and private schools. At boarding school, you live with the faculty and other students. Usually, boarding school students are required to participate in sports or other activities, and joining football teams can be wonderful experiences for the players. Boarding school games offer a different atmosphere than typical high school games. Games are often played on Saturday afternoons rather than Friday nights. The players are from all over, so there's not usually a crowd of local supporters, but the student section is enthusiastic. Schools broadcast their games over the Internet so that the faraway parents and alumni can follow along.

game, in which the starters and the scout team play a shortened version of a real game, complete with a coin toss, kickoffs, and coaches pretending to be referees.

Thursday's practice before a Friday night game is usually a relaxed practice. The players are storing up their energy for the next day's game. They don't want to get banged up or sore without time to recover. But the players can still run through their plays, and they generally go through the motions of beating the opponent. By the end of Thursday's practice, the team will be ready for the game.

State Championships

High school teams play eight to eleven regular season games. Just like college teams are members of a conference, high school teams play many of their games against the same schools every year. In high school, this group of schools is usually called a district, though the term is different in some states. The regular season schedule usually includes one game against each of the other teams in the same district. Districts are chosen to include similar-sized schools from the same local area.

At season's end, the best team or teams in the district advance to the state playoffs. Though big and small schools might play regular season games against each other, in the playoffs, teams only play schools of about the same size. The state association sets up tournaments similar to the college Division II and Division III playoffs. The winner of each playoff game advances to the next round. Eventually, the remaining teams are from different parts of the state. The championship games—one in each size category—are often held in a major college or NFL stadium because of the huge crowds that show up.

CHAPTER 6

Offensive Football

Where's the Player?

Break the Last to First code to read this silly riddle and its silly answer!

hatW si het ifferenced etweenb a ootballf layerp nda a uckd?

ou'llY indf neo ni a uddleh, nda het thero ni a uddlep!

What Is the Offense?

The offense is the group of players on a football team that tries to carry the ball into the end zone. They can use all sorts of different plays and strategies to move the ball. At its heart, though, every play is either a running play or a passing play.

Running Plays

On running plays, the quarterback usually hands the ball to a running back. Sometimes the quarterback will keep the ball and run it. Either way, on running plays the offensive line tries to push the defensive team back in order to give the runner holes to run through. Running plays will usually gain a few yards. It's unlikely that a team will lose yards running the ball, but it's also unlikely that they'll make big gains. Running is especially important for a team that is trying to hold on to a lead because the clock will almost always keep counting down after a running play.

Passing Plays

On passing plays, the quarterback holds the ball and tries to throw it to one of his receivers. The offensive line doesn't push down the field; rather, it drops back and tries to keep the defensive team away from the quarterback. Passing plays are riskier than running plays—passes can be intercepted, and the offense doesn't gain any yards if a pass isn't caught. But passes are also the way to make big gains.

A good offense is balanced and includes both passing and running plays. Sure, some teams use one type of play more than the other, depending on their players' strengths. But every team must be able to both pass and run.

The precise design of passing and running plays has changed a lot over the past century. Today, teams use all sorts of offensive schemes. A later section of this chapter explains some of the possible strategies that an offense can use. All successful offenses use the same basic types of players: a clever quarterback, a strong offensive line, and powerful or fast receivers and running backs. The first part of this chapter will explain the jobs of each type of player.

The Quarterback

The quarterback is the boss on the field. At the start of pretty much every play, the quarterback gets the ball, and he starts the action. Different offensive schemes may require the quarterback to do different things with the ball. For example, an option-based offense might have the quarterback run the ball (or at least pretend to run the ball) on every play. Most NFL offenses have the quarterback drop back five to seven steps on every play, each time either handing the ball to a running back or passing from the pocket.

Adjusting the Play

During a football game, the coach usually tells the quarterback what kind of play to run. But once the teams have lined up, the quarterback has to decide whether that play is likely to work. For example, imagine that the coach calls a running play to the right side. The quarterback should notice how the defense lines up. If the defense has a lot of players waiting on the right, where the running back is supposed to go, then the quarterback should make the decision to change the play.

WORDS TO KNOW

POCKET: When the quarterback has dropped back to pass, his offensive line forms a horseshoe-shaped pocket around him. They push the pass rushers toward the sideline and down the field, keeping the area around the quarterback clear of defenders until the quarterback can throw a pass.

Football GREAT

Joe Montana

Joe Cool, as he became known, started his career with the San Francisco 49ers in 1979. In only his third year, he led the 49ers to their best NFL season ever: a 13-3 record and a playoff berth. Joe was named the most valuable player in three of his four Super Bowl victories. Throughout his career, Montana was known for his grace under pressure. Twenty-six times he led the 49ers to come-from-behind wins. That's where the nickname Joe Cool came from. Even when his team trailed, they believed Joe could lead them back.

* * The Silly Answer Is * * "The One in the Sugar Bowl"

What's the silly question? To find out, use the directions to cross words out of the grid. Read the remaining words from left to right and top to bottom.

Cross Out

... *sports that use nets*   ... *places to keep clothes*
... *two-letter words without I*   ... *insects that don't fly*

IF	TENNIS	TWO	ANTS
ON	FLIES	ARE	BASKETBALL
EARWIGS	CLOSET	AN	FLEAS
IN	VOLLEYBALL	THE	DRESSER
SPIDERS	KITCHEN	HAMPER	WHICH
AT	ONE	ROACHES	UP
IS	OR	THE	PING-PONG
BADMINTON	FOOTBALL	OF	PLAYER

One way to change a play is to use code words. Right before the snap, you'll see the quarterback shouting signals to his team. Often, those signals don't mean anything. But everyone on the team knows a few special words for plays. When the quarterback uses those code words, then everyone knows to ignore the play the coach called and instead to run a new play. The code words the quarterback uses are called audibles.

Sometimes the quarterback has options to avoid a stacked defense even after the play starts. The simplest example is that the quarterback might choose to keep the ball and run the other way if a running back is about to run into a blitzing linebacker. A more complicated example is that if he sees a blitz coming, the quarterback can throw to the "hot" receiver.

The Quarterback Who Can Throw Sidearm: Patrick Mahomes

Kansas City Chiefs quarterback Patrick Mahomes was named Super Bowl MVP twice. His father was also a professional athlete—he pitched for the Minnesota Twins for eleven years. Patrick has an extremely strong arm, just like his father. Sometimes, Patrick will run out of the pocket and throw the ball sidearm-style. Most quarterbacks don't do this because they'd throw way too many interceptions—it's hard to be accurate sidearm, and it's so easy to miss seeing a defender when throwing across the field. Patrick Mahomes, though, usually completes seemingly impossible passes this way.

Mahomes has been the Chiefs' starting quarterback since 2018, when he was the NFL's most valuable player—in his first year as a starter! He then led the team to six straight AFC championship games and two Super Bowl victories.

Football GREAT

Lamar Jackson

In 2016, as a sophomore, Louisville quarterback Lamar Jackson won the Heisman Trophy. Known for his ability to run as well as to pass, Jackson decided to skip his senior year and enter the NFL draft, expecting to become an NFL quarterback. Some football draft "experts" said that Lamar Jackson could never be a quarterback in the NFL and that he would only be successful as a wide receiver.

But what did they know? Jackson was a first-round pick who led the Baltimore Ravens to the playoffs in his rookie year, and a total of five times in seven seasons. And Jackson won both the 2019 and 2023 NFL most valuable player awards, in 2019 on a unanimous vote. Seems like he didn't need to move to wide receiver after all!

Tom Brady: The Greatest of All Time?

Tom Brady was an extremely accomplished college quarterback. However, he was not picked in the first round of the NFL draft in 2000. Nope, 198 players were chosen before he was. Most of those teams that passed on him now regret their decision, as Brady had tremendous success with the New England Patriots. In nineteen full seasons as a starter, he led the Patriots to nine Super Bowls, winning six of them (and earning the MVP trophy in four of them). He later won his fifth Super Bowl MVP with the Tampa Bay Buccaneers. His teams have always won more than they lost; he won nearly 80 percent of the games he started, including an undefeated 16-0 regular season in 2007.

Brady is best known for his playoff successes. Like his idol Joe Montana, Tom repeatedly authored game-winning drives in crucial games. He won thirty-four playoff games; the next-closest quarterback only won thirteen. He was just as good or better under the intense pressure of a playoff game as he was in the first game of the season. Brady retired after the 2022 season, celebrating a career that spanned parts of three decades.

The Offensive Line

A team's offensive linemen are the men who move mountains. They have one job: to block the defense. On running plays, they open up lanes for running backs to run through. On passing plays, they protect the quarterback by forming a pocket. It takes a special kind of unselfish person to be an offensive lineman. Fans rarely hear about the linemen, except when they are called for a penalty. Linemen don't usually score touchdowns, don't make tackles, and don't gain yards. Yet the line is the most important unit on the offense. A good offensive line can make a bad running back look great. By giving him time to throw, a good offensive line can make any quarterback who can throw look awesome.

The offensive line consists of the center, who snaps the ball; the two guards, who line up just right and left of the center; and the two offensive tackles, who line up just right and left of the guards.

Running Plays

The first job of the offensive line on a running play is to create a surge. The offensive linemen have an advantage over the defense because they know when the ball will be snapped. When the ball is snapped, the linemen move powerfully in the direction of the play, trying to take two steps before they contact a defender. This process is called firing off the line.

Zone Blocking

Before the snap, all the linemen have to know their responsibilities. They have to know which direction to fire off the line, and they have to know if there's a specific defensive player they're assigned to block.

In zone blocking, the linemen all fire out together in one direction. They block anyone in their way, pushing whichever defender they see. Zone blockers are like trains on a track, knocking down everything in their path and not letting anyone cross. A zone blocker's first responsibility is to block defensive linemen. If no defensive lineman is in the way, the offensive linemen can get to the next level; that is, they can race upfield and block a linebacker. One advantage of zone blocking is that no specific offensive player is assigned to get to the next level. Instead, whichever lineman doesn't have anyone to block can be used effectively.

WORDS TO KNOW

SNAP COUNT: Every play starts when the center snaps the ball to the quarterback. But how does the center know when to snap? The quarterback shouts "Hut!" when he wants the ball. Sometimes, though, the quarterback will shout "Hut, hut!" or even "Hut, hut, hut!" Before every play, the quarterback tells the offense how many times he'll say "Hut" before the snap.

Traps and Pulls

If linemen blocked the same way on every play, the defense would know exactly how to avoid them to make tackles. Traps and pulls are ways for the offense to change strategy to surprise the defense. Guards are usually assigned to trap and pull, but tackles and the center can run these plays just as well.

Imagine a defensive lineman is very fast, so fast that he sometimes beats the offensive player assigned to block him. What can the offense do? Let him get past the offensive line surge. Let the defender think he's going to make a play, but send the tackle from the other side of the field to run behind the line right toward where the defender will be. This tackle blocks the defender sideways and out of the play. Such a play is called a trap because the defender is usually surprised and can't see the tackle coming.

Another way to trick the defense is to pull a guard or tackle into a hole. When the offensive line creates a hole for a running back to run through, the defensive linebackers are coached to get in that hole to stop the running back. To trick the defense, the offense sends the guard from the other side of the field to run into the hole ahead of the running back. The guard blocks the linebacker who thinks they're going to make a play, and the running back can keep running.

Pass Protection

Passing plays are simpler for linemen. Instead of creating a surge, they try to keep the defenders away from the quarterback. They form a pocket by pushing the rushers forward and to the side. Sometimes the linemen have to stand their ground against a bull-rushing defensive lineman. Sometimes, though, it's good enough just to make the defender go away from the quarterback. On passing plays, all that matters is that the quarterback has enough time to throw. Whether defenders are knocked down or pushed aside isn't important.

TRY THIS

Can You Find the Traps and Pulls?

Now that you know a bit about how linemen play, you can look closely for a pulling guard or a trapping tackle. Each time you notice one of these plays, write down what you saw, whether the lineman made the block they were supposed to make, and how many yards the play gained.

Hide the Football

There are ten football words hiding in these sentences. Can you find them all? We've given you a list of words to look for, but watch out — there are extra words in the list!

BLOCK	FOULS	LINE	PUNT	SNAP
CENTER	FUMBLE	PIGSKIN	RUSH	SWEEP
CLOCK	KICK	PLAY	SCORE	TEAM

1. Is the game on one disc or eleven cassettes?
2. We won! Hear us "Hooray!"
3. The champ lay winded in the end zone.
4. The quarterback spun, then threw the ball.
5. Tired players nap before the big game.
6. Don't panic! Lock the stadium door!
7. All I need is to move the ball four more yards!
8. Losing teams weep in private!
9. All of Ray Spigs' kin came to watch him play!
10. Drinking iced tea makes players less thirsty.

Numbering Rules

Offensive linemen are not eligible to catch passes. So everyone can tell who the ineligible linemen are, all offensive linemen must wear a number between 50 and 79. (And anyone who is eligible to catch a pass must wear numbers from 1–49 or 80–99.)

HOT RECEIVER: A blitz is when lots of unexpected defenders rush toward the quarterback. The quarterback has to get rid of the ball quickly! On many passing plays, one receiver runs a very short route, called a hot route, and gets ready to catch the ball right away. If the quarterback sees a blitz, he knows he can throw right away to the hot receiver to avoid being sacked.

The major difficulty in pass protection is picking up a blitz. When the defense sends five or six players, the quarterback is supposed to notice this and throw to the hot receiver. The line still has to give him enough time to make that throw. It's usually most important to block the players coming up the middle because they can get to the quarterback fastest. A tackle who sees a blitz might have to leave their man to help out the guard and center. Often, the running back is assigned to help out the offensive line on a blitz—the running back can block the outside defender that the tackle let go.

In the NFL Today

Tackle Penei Sewell grew up in American Samoa, a United States territory closer to Australia than to the US mainland. He moved to Utah for high school and then played college football at the University of Oregon. He was drafted by the Detroit Lions in 2021 and is the anchor of their offensive line, leading the team to an NFC championship game in 2023.

As left tackle, Sewell protects quarterback Jared Goff's blind side. Sewell is generally assigned to block the opponent's most fearsome pass rusher on each of fifty or so snaps in a game.

The Running Back

It may seem obvious, but the running back's job is to take a handoff from the quarterback and run. Yes, you knew that already, right? The running back has other jobs as well, but by far the most important is to carry the ball.

A good ballcarrier is not only fast but is also quick and able to change directions on the spur of the moment. Strong running backs can make correct decisions about where to run the ball. When the offensive line is zone blocking, it's not clear right away exactly where the best spot to run will be. The running back has to read the blocks. For example, a zone running play might be designed to get the ball outside, toward the sideline. But if the outside defender has pushed outside to stop this play, the running back has to recognize right away to cut straight up the field or back to the middle, wherever the line has opened up space.

Beyond speed, quickness, and decision-making, the running back has to be tough. The running back is probably tackled more times per game than anyone else. A runner who can still gain a few yards after getting hit by a defender is extremely valuable. Running backs who can bounce right up, ready to carry the ball again on the next play, are making an enormous contribution to the offense.

What else do running backs have to do besides run? First of all, they often have to block on passing plays. Especially if the defense sends a blitz, the running back has to be aware of any rushers that the offensive line might miss.

An Old-Style Running Back: Christian McCaffrey

In the twentieth century, a team would usually have one star running back who carried the ball two hundred, three hundred, or more times in a season. Nowadays, teams will use several running backs in a game, often using different players for rushing, blocking, and pass catching. Christian McCaffrey, however, has been a top running back in *all* of these roles for many years. He helped lead the Panthers to the playoffs in his rookie season. The 49ers traded for McCaffrey in 2022 and were rewarded with six playoff games in two years, a 300-carry, 1,500-yard season in 2023, and 160 all-purpose yards in Super Bowl LVIII.

WORDS TO KNOW

ELIGIBLE RECEIVERS: On every play, the offense must line up seven players on the line of scrimmage. The middle five of these players may not catch a pass. Only players on the end of this line are eligible receivers. Players who line up behind the line of scrimmage are also eligible receivers.

Football GREAT

Walter Payton

Walter "Sweetness" Payton played for thirteen years, from 1975 to 1987. In 1975, the Bears drafted him with their first pick. Walter set eight NFL records in his career, including the most rushing yards in a single game, most career rushing yards, and most career total yards. Walter Payton remains perhaps the most-loved Bear in team history.

The Wide Receiver

The receiver's main job is possibly the simplest to understand: Get open, catch the ball, and then run with the ball.

Get Open

On each passing play, a receiver is assigned a route to run. The route tells the receiver which way to run and when to change directions. The receiver and the quarterback will practice that route hundreds of times so the quarterback will have an idea of when and where to throw the ball. It's the receiver's job to run the route full speed, the same way he ran it in practice, to make it easier for the quarterback to read whether the receiver is open.

Depending on the defense, sometimes a receiver has to adjust the route. For example, it's a bad idea to run right into a defender's zone (an area of the field the defender is responsible for) because then the receiver would be covered easily. Against a zone defense, the receiver might need to stop his route early to stay open. On the other hand, against a man-to-man defense, the receiver should keep running past his defender, or he might need to adjust his route away from his defender.

Catch the Ball

This may sound like an obvious skill not even worthy of mention. But there's nothing more frustrating to an offense than the perfect pass thrown to an open receiver who drops the ball. On the other hand, there's nothing more exciting or inspiring than an outstanding catch. A receiver must work to develop good hands—yes, hands—because the ball should always be caught with the hands, not cradled against the body. Receivers can practice diving for a catch or catching balls that are thrown off target or with a lot of force. The more

WORDS TO KNOW

BALL SECURITY: All of the great running in the world is useless if the running back fumbles the ball. Defenders not only try to tackle the ballcarrier; they also try to take the ball away. By carrying the ball properly and covering the ball with two hands when about to be hit, the running back can protect the team's possession.

DUMP-OFF: When the offensive line forms a pocket and the receivers run downfield, the defense is ready for a long pass. Sometimes they forget about the running back. In one common dump-off pass, the running back and some linemen pretend to miss their blocks so the pass rushers think they can tackle the quarterback. Then the quarterback throws a short pass over the rushers to the running back, who now has a clear field in front of him for a long gain.

experience someone has catching difficult passes, the more likely that person is to make the tough catch in the game.

Run!

As soon as receivers catch the ball, they must tuck the ball away like a running back. Ball security should be the first priority. Then they have to get that ball upfield. Receivers who have caught the ball are usually far away from the biggest defenders. If they can beat one or two tacklers, they might score a touchdown.

Blocking

Even the best receivers don't get the ball thrown to them more than ten or so times per game. Truly great receivers help their team win on every play, though.

On running plays, a receiver will usually have a blocking assignment. No, they won't have to block that 320-pound nose tackle, but they might have to block a linebacker or safety so the running back can run toward the sideline. Receivers should learn proper blocking form, especially because they often weigh less than the people they're supposed to block. Fortunately, it's not necessary to knock a defender down on every play. Just getting in the way and making some physical contact is often enough. But the stronger a blocker you are, the farther away from you the cornerbacks might play, letting you take advantage of them on a passing play!

Chris Carter's Heir

Adam Thielen grew up in Minnesota idolizing famous Vikings receiver Chris Carter. He played college football at Minnesota State, and then he played for the Minnesota Vikings for ten years. He was selected to the Pro Bowl in 2017 and 2018. In eleven years in the NFL, he's only missed nine games. His team has averaged 9 yards per target—that's not

Football GREAT

Jerry Rice

Jerry Rice played for sixteen years with the 49ers and another four years with the Raiders and Seahawks. He was the greatest receiver ever to play. He led the league six times in receiving yards and touchdown receptions, retiring with the most receiving yardage of anyone in NFL history. Jerry played in four Super Bowls—three with the 49ers and one with the Raiders—catching a touchdown in each game and earning the MVP trophy for Super Bowl XXIII.

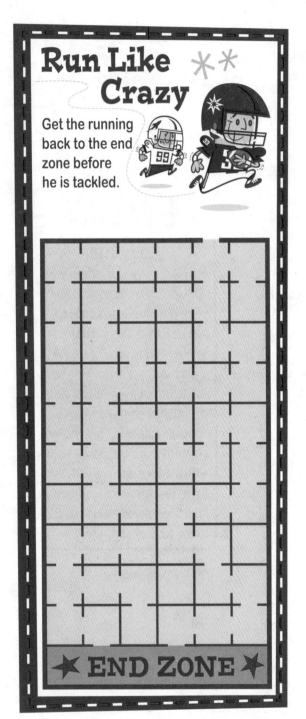

Run Like Crazy ✳ ✳

Get the running back to the end zone before he is tackled.

★ END ZONE ★

9 yards per catch, that's an average of 9 yards every time they throw the ball in his direction! Thielen joined the Carolina Panthers in 2023, catching 100 passes for 1,000 yards, yet again putting him among the NFL's best receivers.

Offensive Schemes: Formations and Methods of Attack

Way back at the beginning of football, the rules didn't allow forward passes. Every play had to be a running play. The defense had an easier time because there was no need to defend the deep part of the field.

Single-Wing Formation

Even after the forward pass was made legal from anywhere behind the line of scrimmage in 1933, football was still a running game. Plays were designed for blockers to open holes for running backs. In the single-wing formation, the stack of two wingbacks (running backs positioned behind a tight end) and a fullback (a running back mainly used as a blocker) helped the offensive linemen block. The quarterback took the snap 5 yards in the backfield and usually ran behind his blockers on the strong side of the formation.

T Formation

The T formation became widespread beginning in the late 1930s. In the T, the quarterback took the snap under center with his running backs behind him. This was an improvement over the single wing because the quarterback could hand off to any of the running backs, which meant the defense couldn't predict who would carry the ball. Furthermore, passing became easier in the T. If the quarterback faked a handoff, he would be in a good position to throw a pass.

The Passing Game

As passing became a more important part of offensive football, receivers (called split ends or flankers) began lining up farther away from the center. This forced the defense to move players away from the middle of the field to cover the receivers, opening up the running game as well as the passing game. The modern "pro set" eventually evolved from the T formation: two running backs behind the quarterback (under center), a tight end (part lineman, part receiver, the tight end lines up next to the tackle but is eligible to receive a pass), a flanker, and a wide receiver.

Option Offense

When a team has an athletic quarterback who has not developed into a first-rate passer, they might choose to run an option offense. In this run-based offense, the quarterback runs, intending to pitch the ball to a running back who trails behind them. If the defense covers the running back, though, the quarterback has the option to keep the ball and run upfield. Many college teams of the 1960s and 1970s used the "wishbone" offense, in which three running backs gave the quarterback a triple option. Option offenses may only throw three or four passes per game, but these can be so surprising to the defense that they result in long gains.

West Coast Offense

In high-level college football and in the NFL, the quarterback is usually not the best athlete on the field but instead is a deadly accurate thrower and an excellent decision-maker. The goal of these offenses is for the quarterback to evaluate the

Receivers Win the Game with Blocking!

Late in the 1988 AFC championship game, the Cincinnati Bengals were driving for a touchdown against the Buffalo Bills. A 15-yard penalty saved the Bengals' drive and gave them the winning score. What happened? Well, all day long the Bengals receivers had been blocking hard on every running play, even when the play was not in their direction. All these blocks were clean but tough. Finally, one of the Bills defenders got mad and shoved the Bengals receiver after the play, earning a penalty and allowing the Bengals to score a touchdown.

LATERAL: The rules about forward passes are very strict. But any player can throw a backward pass at any time. A backward pass is often called a lateral.

WORDS TO KNOW

DRAW PLAY: Imagine your team faces third down and has 9 yards to go, so the defense expects a pass. The offensive line sets up to form a pocket, the quarterback drops back to pass, and the receivers run pass routes. But wait! Instead of throwing, the quarterback hands the ball to a running back, fooling everyone and allowing a long gain! That fake pass that turns into a run is called a draw play.

defense and get the ball to a great athlete who has room to run. For example, the West Coast offense is a passing offense, but it pays more attention to short rather than long passes. The strategy is to throw the ball quickly to open receivers 5–10 yards downfield. These receivers can sometimes break for long runs after the catch. Even if they can't, eventually defenders can be fooled into allowing a deep pass or a long run.

Sam Wyche and the No-Huddle Offense

In 1988, Cincinnati Bengals coach Sam Wyche realized that his team could gain an offensive advantage by running quickly to the line of scrimmage after every play. That way, the defense couldn't substitute as they got tired, and they wouldn't have time to discuss their coverages or blitz schemes. Wyche's team practiced their communication—they had all sorts of code words to call plays quickly while the team was already lined up. Today, many college and pro teams run a version of the no-huddle offense, and substitution rules have changed so that the defense is given time to match up. But it's still a big advantage to have an offense that can call and run plays quickly!

Spread Offense

Today, many college teams have found success with a "spread offense." A spread team usually lines up a running back and a shotgun quarterback—a quarterback who lines up several yards behind the center to receive the snap—in the backfield, and four receivers line up across the field far apart from each other. Because the receivers and even the linemen are spread out so far along the line of scrimmage, the defense also has to spread out. The quarterback can decide who to throw the ball to or whether to run the ball by recognizing how the defense has lined up and reading how the defense reacts to the start of the play.

NFL teams take a spread offense one step further. An NFL offense often has to fool the defense by disguising what they're trying to do. If they can make a defender take even one step the wrong way, they can manage a big gain. Nowadays, NFL teams use multiple formations. They might run the same pass to their best receiver several times in a game. But if that receiver starts each play in a different spot on the field, the defense never knows what to expect.

The Read Option and the Run-Pass Option

Read option means that the quarterback has the option to give the ball to the running back or to keep the ball himself. To make that decision, the quarterback reads what the defensive end is doing. If the end chases after the running back, then the quarterback keeps the ball and runs right past the end. However, if the end stays put to try to tackle the quarterback, then the quarterback sticks the ball in the running back's belly, and the running back has one less player in position to tackle him.

In a standard running play, the quarterback just hands the ball off, so the defense doesn't have to pay any attention to him. A read option makes the defense account for one extra player. The "run-pass option," or RPO, similarly relies on the quarterback deciding what to do based on one defender's movement. But the RPO gives the quarterback the option of throwing a quick pass to take advantage of where the defender goes.

Option offenses are difficult to stop if they're executed well. Unless every defender is in exactly the right place, and unless the defense refuses to be fooled, option runs and short passes can turn into very long gains.

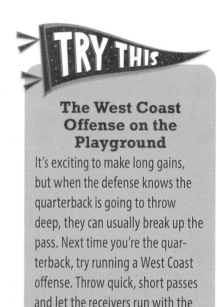

TRY THIS

The West Coast Offense on the Playground

It's exciting to make long gains, but when the defense knows the quarterback is going to throw deep, they can usually break up the pass. Next time you're the quarterback, try running a West Coast offense. Throw quick, short passes and let the receivers run with the ball. You'll end up frustrating the defense, and you'll probably win the game.

WORDS TO KNOW

FLEA FLICKER: This silly-sounding name describes a common trick play. The quarterback hands the ball to the running back, who runs toward the line of scrimmage, but before he reaches the line of scrimmage or any defenders, the running back throws the ball backward to the quarterback! Usually a receiver is open deep downfield because the defenders saw the handoff and expected a running play.

Football GREAT

Barry Sanders

Barry played running back for the Detroit Lions for ten seasons, from 1989–1998. He led the NFL in rushing four times and went to the Pro Bowl every single season. Barry didn't bowl over the defense—rather, he spun and left defenders grabbing at air as he whooshed by. His long runs and numerous touchdowns made him one of history's best players to own on a fantasy team. In 1999, Barry retired, and the Lions have had only seven winning seasons since.

Fooling the Defense

Sometimes, the offense tries to trick the defense. Sometimes the trickery is obvious to everyone when it happens, as when the quarterback fakes a handoff and throws the ball instead. But just as often, a play works because of an acting job by a player you may not have noticed, like a receiver who pretends to block before running a pass route or a tight end who falls down only to get up to catch a pass.

A defense isn't tricked easily. The offense must first establish patterns that they can later break. For example, a wide receiver might run a post pattern (a route that angles toward the goalpost) on each of the first fifteen passing plays, even if the quarterback doesn't throw to that receiver. But on the sixteenth play, the receiver might fake the post and instead run toward the sideline deep downfield. The defenders won't be expecting that, and they may not be able to react right away. The receiver will be wide open for a long gain or a touchdown.

Receivers must run hard on every play, even when they know they're not going to get the ball. Linemen have to use the same stance for every play. They have to be careful not to give away whether they'll be pass blocking or run blocking. A real handoff should look the same as a fake handoff—the running back should run toward the line of scrimmage, and the quarterback should prepare to pass, no matter who actually has the ball. If all eleven players on a team do their jobs, then a few times in every game the offense should be able to make gains on tricky plays.

CHAPTER 7

Defensive Football

Defense! Defense!

Watch Lavonte David wrestle a running back to the ground, T.J. Watt burst past the offensive linemen to take down a quarterback, and Charvarius Ward snatch a ball out of the air for an interception. They make it look easy, but all three of these defensive players have the smarts to read the offense's plays and the physical strength to make sure they don't succeed.

The Basics

The eleven defensive players line up opposite the offense with one mission—keep the offense from scoring. At first, defensive strategy seems much simpler than offensive strategy: Just tackle anyone who tries to run the ball while covering the receivers to be sure they can't catch a pass. But since the offense is always trying to confuse and trick the defense, the defense must disguise who covers whom, and they must adjust their strategies from play to play so they don't become predictable.

Keys to Successful Defense

Regardless of the specific scheme a team runs, the defense uses three kinds of players: defensive linemen, linebackers, and the cornerbacks and safeties who together are called the secondary. In this chapter, you'll first learn about the jobs done by each of these positions, then you'll find a discussion of the 4-3 and the 3-4 defenses and how they differ. You'll learn how zone defenses work. When you've read this chapter, you'll be able to understand most of what the announcers at a football game are talking about when they describe a team's defense.

Super Bowl Defensive MVPs

Ten defensive players have been named Super Bowl MVP. The most recent was Von Miller, the Broncos linebacker, in 2016. Only one special team's player, Green Bay's Desmond Howard in Super Bowl XXXI, has ever received the honor.

The Defensive Line

Teams use either three or four defensive linemen. The biggest and strongest of these players line up in the middle of the formation, across from the center and the guards. These are called the defensive tackles. The player who lines up directly across from the center is the nose tackle. The tackles have only one job, but it's an important one: Give a couple of offensive linemen someone to block. If two offensive players have to block one defensive lineman, then the other defensive players have a better chance of making a play.

Every defensive tackle tries to make two blockers block him to free up space for the linebackers to make a tackle. Mean Joe Greene's rush was so powerful and his alignment so unpredictable that he would often take up three blockers. Under his leadership, the Steelers' "Steel Curtain" defense dominated the league for at least a decade.

The defensive linemen on the outside of the formation are called the defensive ends. On running plays, they have a similar job to the defensive tackles: If they can't make the play themselves, they try to occupy two blockers so that someone else is free to tackle the ballcarrier. On passing plays, though, the defensive ends have a one-track mind: Get the quarterback. Ideally, they'll tackle the quarterback for a sack. If they can't, they need to hurry the quarterback and make him throw a pass before he's ready. Sometimes the defensive ends can put their arms up and knock down a pass. In any case, the defensive ends must be fast and quick to get around the offensive linemen blocking them and to get to the quarterback as soon as possible. The sooner they bother the quarterback, the shorter the time that the secondary has to cover the receivers and the more likely it is that a quarterback will throw an incomplete or intercepted pass.

Football GREAT

Mean Joe Green

Teams at the University of North Texas (formerly known as North Texas State University) are nicknamed the Mean Green. When Charles Edward Greene showed up in the 1960s, everyone called him Mean Joe Greene. Joe carried this name with him to the Pittsburgh Steelers, where he played defensive tackle for thirteen seasons and helped his team win four Super Bowls. He was NFL defensive player of the year twice, went to ten Pro Bowls, and was named to the NFL All-Pro team eight times.

Purple People Eaters

The Minnesota Vikings went to four Super Bowls in the 1960s and 1970s. They were a dominant team during that time, largely due to their awe-inspiring defensive line: tackles Alan Page, Gary Larsen, and Doug Sutherland, and ends Carl "Moose" Eller and Jim Marshall. Their motto was "Meet at the quarterback." This defensive line earned the nickname the Purple People Eaters. To a quarterback, they must have looked like an enormous chewing monster in purple uniforms.

Nick Bosa of the 49ers is one of the best defensive ends in the game today. This 2019 first-round pick has intimidated quarterbacks and offensive linemen with his explosive pass rush and his strength playing the run. Opponents often double-team Bosa, giving teammates like linebacker Fred Warner opportunities to make plays. But Bosa usually manages to fight through that double team, evidenced by the fact that he's averaged nearly a sack per game in his career.

The Linebacker

The first job of a linebacker is to stop the run. At the snap, they all take a read step toward the line of scrimmage. While they step, they watch the offensive linemen. If the offensive linemen block for a running play, then the read step gives the linebacker momentum to fill whatever gap opens up for the running back to come through. It's the linebackers' job to run wherever necessary to stop the running back. That means knowing which gap between offensive players they're responsible for, but also knowing who has the ball in order to react to the play. It also means using their hands to keep offensive players from blocking them.

If the linemen set up to pass block, then the linebackers drop back into pass coverage. Most of the time, linebackers will be responsible for stopping receivers who run short routes across the field. Sometimes a linebacker will be assigned to watch the running backs in case they come out of the backfield to catch a pass. The specific coverage assignment depends on the team's defensive strategy. That strategy may include linebacker blitzes, where a linebacker rushes the quarterback once they read a pass play.

Most Valuable Player

What kind of football career will this player have? To figure out what the coach tells him, fill in the blanks with the numbered words.

Hey, Coach! I want to play 1 _____ , 2 _____ , and 3 _____ !

OK — 4 _____ at the 1 _____ of the 7 _____ , 2 _____ the 6 _____ 8 _____ , and 3 _____ 9 _____ who gets 5 _____ it!

6 WATER

7 BENCH

2 GUARD

1 END

4 SIT

5 NEAR

3 TACKLE

8 BUCKET

9 ANYONE

Football GREAT

Mike Singletary

Mike Singletary played for twelve seasons as the Chicago Bears' middle linebacker, making the Pro Bowl team ten times and the All-Pro team nine times, and twice being named the defensive player of the year. With Mike Singletary in the middle of the defense, the Bears used a new, aggressive defense called the 46. The idea was to blitz all the time and from all different directions. The pinnacle of his career came in the 1985 season: In the Super Bowl XX game, Mike recovered two fumbles, and his top-rated defense led the Bears to a dominant 46–10 victory.

Communication

The linebackers serve key roles as communicators for the defense. Before the snap, the defensive linemen don't have a good view of the offensive formation because they are trying to get in a low-to-the-ground stance. The linebackers have to tell them what they see: Which is the strong side of the offense, where there are more players? How many runners are in the backfield? Should the defense change its strategy? The linebackers will usually communicate this information using some sort of code words so the offense can't catch on.

Making the Tackle

More than anyone else on the defense, the linebackers are in charge of tackling. The defensive linemen try to force the running back to where the linebackers can make a tackle. Good linebackers are not only fast enough to get where they're supposed to be; they're strong too, with outstanding tackling form: head up, legs driving, arms wrapping the ballcarrier in a bear hug as they fall to the ground. Sure, all defensive players should be good tacklers, but the linebackers have to be the best.

The Best Tackler

Lavonte David was not highly recruited out of high school, though his Miami-area team won two straight Florida state championships behind his leadership. Even after an outstanding college career at Middle Tennessee State and Nebraska, people said he was too small to play linebacker in the NFL. They were, um, wrong. Eight years into his career, he has more tackles than all but four active players, whether you count solo tackles or combined tackles. He's topped one hundred tackles in seven of those years. He forces fumbles at an amazing rate; he's recovered more fumbles than any Tampa Bay Buccaneer in history. David was named to the NFL's "all-decade" team for the 2010s.

The Secondary

Together, the cornerbacks and safeties are called defensive backs, or the secondary. Whereas the first job of the linebackers is to stop the run, the first job of the defensive backs is to cover receivers.

The Safeties

The safeties line up deep in the backfield, 10–15 yards from the line of scrimmage. The strong safety lines up to the tight end's side of the formation, while the free safety lines up opposite the strong safety. At the snap, the safeties watch the tight end and the other linemen to quickly find out whether the play will be a run or pass. On a running play, the safeties, especially the strong safety, come toward the line in run support. They aid the linebackers in bringing down running backs. Safeties are usually a bit less aggressive in plugging holes because they are the last line of defense. If a linebacker misses a tackle, there's more help, but if a safety gets out of position, the cost is likely a touchdown.

The safety's main job, though, is pass coverage. The safety is usually responsible for a deep zone. Once the safeties recognize a passing play, they find the receiver most likely to threaten their area of the field—that's usually the tight end or the slot receiver (the receiver lined up between the last player on the offensive line and the wide receiver). The safety reads this receiver's route, preparing to cover them if they stay in the safety's zone.

The safeties can't focus exclusively on this one player, though. At the same time, they have to be aware of what the outside receiver is doing, even though the outside receiver is at first the cornerback's responsibility. If two receivers run crossing routes, the safety and cornerback must notice, and they should switch coverage, usually with the safety taking the deeper route.

Help from the Sideline

As soon as it's clear whether a play is a running or passing play, every player on the sideline yells "Run!" or "Pass!" On a passing play, as soon as the quarterback throws the ball, the sideline yells "Ball!" Linebackers and defensive backs make their own reads, but they can and do use the sideline's call to help them out.

Heisman Winner

Only one defensive player has ever won college football's coveted Heisman Trophy—Michigan cornerback Charles Woodson in 1997. He beat out a strong field that included Tennessee quarterback Peyton Manning and Marshall University wide receiver Randy Moss. Charles was drafted by the Oakland Raiders and was named the 1998 defensive rookie of the year. He retired in 2015, after eighteen years in Oakland and Green Bay, nine Pro Bowls, and one Super Bowl ring.

Football GREAT

Darrell Green

In 1983, the Washington team chose cornerback Darrell Green in the first round. He played for Washington for twenty years. In three championship games, Darrell caught an interception and scored a touchdown on a punt return. Offenses like to run big running backs to the outside, daring the smaller cornerback to make a difficult tackle. Darrell's presence could not only shut down a receiver on his side of the field; it could also force the offense to run to the other side of the field. Green was voted into the NFL Hall of Fame in 2008.

Safeties aren't always in a deep zone. A safety could be part of double coverage on a dangerous receiver. They could be asked to scoot up to stop a team that's been running a lot, leaving pass coverage to the cornerbacks. Or they could rush the quarterback on a safety blitz. Safeties have to be athletic players to fill all of these roles.

The Cornerbacks

Cornerbacks line up on the corners of the formation, in front of the widest receivers. Corners will help out on running plays, usually by attempting to force a ballcarrier back to the inside where the linebackers are waiting for him. Yet the cornerbacks must play the pass first. If the cornerback makes the mistake of looking to see whether the quarterback handed off, a receiver will run by. The general rule for cornerbacks is to defend as if the quarterback will throw the ball until the sideline calls "Run!"

A cornerback always has to know where the safeties are supposed to be. For example, are the corners supposed to cover short routes, with the safeties playing deep? Or will the safety cover inside routes, with the corner taking the outside and deep routes? Knowing where the safeties are will tell the cornerback how to cover a receiver. The cornerback should cover any route that the safety won't be able to get to.

Jamming the Receiver

Passing offenses rely on precise routes and practiced timing between the quarterback and receivers. One of the best ways to disrupt an offense is for the cornerbacks to jam the receivers right after the snap. In high school and college, defenders can bump a receiver until the ball is thrown. Unless the cornerback is supposed to cover the deep part of the field, it's useful to give the receiver a bump. But if the cornerback misses when trying to jam, the receiver could be wide open.

The Two Major Defensive Alignments

Most teams organize their defense in one of two ways. The 3-4 defense uses three defensive linemen and four linebackers, while the 4-3 defense uses four defensive linemen and three linebackers. There are advantages and disadvantages to each. Most of the time, the choice of which scheme to use depends on the players a team has to fill the positions.

The majority of NFL teams use the 4-3. Four linemen make it easier to keep the offensive line busy. Even though there are only three linebackers, they are more likely to be free to make a play. In a 4-3, each of the three linebackers has their own job:

- The strong-side linebacker, called "Sam," lines up on the tight end's side of the field. Since the offense is more likely to run toward the tight end, Sam is likely to be the person in place to stop a running back.
- The weak-side linebacker, called "Will," lines up opposite the tight end. He has to be a bit faster than Sam because he more often has to cross the whole field to make a play. Since Will is pretty fast, he is used in pass coverage more often than Sam.
- The middle linebacker, called "Mike," is the captain of the defense. Mike is usually the player who communicates with the coaches and then runs the huddle to tell his teammates the play. Mike's position in the middle lets him read running plays quickly. By seeing where the ballcarrier is probably headed, Mike can often be the first one there to make the tackle. A speedy middle linebacker is often used in pass coverage. Especially when the two safeties are sitting in deep coverage, the Mike linebacker has to be ready to cover the tight end over the middle of the field.

WORDS TO KNOW

CROSSING ROUTES: In a zone defense, defenders cover an area of the field. Crossing routes try to confuse the defenders about which receivers are in their area. A simple set of crossing routes could have the receivers cut in front of one another, trading sides of the field. Or a receiver could start on a deep route but pull up short while a teammate runs by into the deep zone.

ON AN ISLAND: A cornerback is often responsible for covering the same receiver through most of the game. The corner will have help from a safety for many plays, but sometimes they will be in true "man-to-man" coverage. In that case, the cornerback is said to be "on an island"—all alone, far away from anyone else, with no help in sight.

A 3-4 defense uses these same three linebackers, plus one more inside linebacker. Usually on pass plays, one of the four linebackers will rush the quarterback with the defensive linemen. An advantage of the 3-4 is that the offensive line never knows which linebacker will be rushing.

Defensive Strategies

The scheme, whether 4-3 or 3-4, is a description of how a team lines up and what roles each player fills. All defenses, regardless of their overall scheme, use pass-rushing strategies, while the secondary uses man and zone coverage, sometimes in combination.

Blitz!

In playground football, a player who doesn't count to seven before rushing the quarterback is said to blitz. The number of blitzes is limited to, say, once every four downs. Since regular football does not require the defense to count before rushing, the term blitz takes on a different meaning.

A defense normally sends four players to rush the quarterback. These are the four defensive linemen. In a 3-4 defense, it's the three linemen and (usually) the Sam linebacker. In a blitz, a fifth or even a sixth player also rushes the quarterback. That's all there is to it.

The obvious advantage of sending a blitz is that the offensive line is outnumbered, so the quarterback has less time to throw a pass before being tackled. But at the same time, the defense has fewer players left to cover the receivers. If the quarterback does manage to throw a pass, a blitz makes it much easier to find an open receiver who can run a long way down the field after catching the ball.

FUN FACT

Zone Blitz

In a zone blitz, a linebacker rushes the quarterback, but one of the defensive linemen doesn't rush. Instead, the lineman drops back in pass coverage, taking over the linebacker's responsibilities. The zone blitz can confuse the quarterback into throwing an interception. But you could argue that a zone blitz isn't even a blitz! Only four players rush the quarterback.

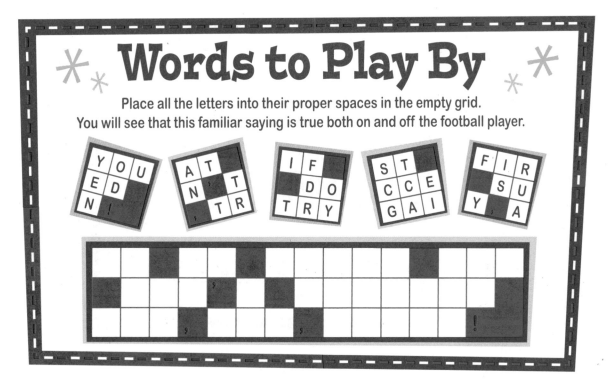

Words to Play By

Place all the letters into their proper spaces in the empty grid.
You will see that this familiar saying is true both on and off the football player.

The most common blitz technique calls for a linebacker to rush in between two defensive linemen. A safety can also blitz and can get more of a running start because safeties line up farther from the line of scrimmage, but it will take a bit longer to reach the quarterback and make it extra difficult to cover the receivers. Occasionally you'll even see a corner blitz, when a cornerback lines up as if to cover a receiver but instead sprints toward the quarterback at the snap.

Stunt

The stunt is a way to confuse the offensive linemen. Normally, the defensive linemen and linebackers rush straight ahead, trying to get into a gap between offensive players. In a stunt, two linemen or linebackers trade places so that they don't attack straight ahead. For example, the nose tackle might run outside the defensive end, hoping that the offense can't figure out who should block them. In that case, a linebacker

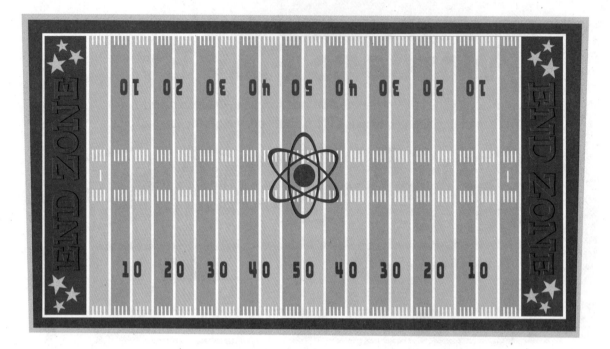

or another defensive lineman would probably move to cover the area where the nose tackle is normally supposed to be.

A stunt is a bit of a gamble. If the offense doesn't adjust, the stunt can lead to a sack or a tackle for a huge loss. But if the offense recognizes the stunt and knows what to do about it, they might be able to take advantage for a big gain.

Different Types of Zone Defense

On most passing plays, the defensive backs will play zone coverage. The most common basic zone defense is called the Cover 2. In this scheme, the safeties play deep and each is in charge of half the width of the field, while the cornerbacks and linebackers defend against short passes. If you're watching a game, you can recognize the Cover 2 by watching where the defensive backs line up at the snap. The two safeties will both be about 15 yards downfield, and the cornerbacks will play close to the wide receivers.

One disadvantage to the Cover 2 is that the offense has an easier time running the ball because both safeties are so far back. If the defense needs to change strategy to stop the run, they can switch to the Cover 3. In this scheme, the strong safety plays close to the line of scrimmage, while the deep part of the field is split into three zones for the free safety and the two cornerbacks. To recognize Cover 3, look for a single deep safety. The cornerbacks will play 5 yards or so away from the receivers so that they can get to their deep third of the field.

Though Cover 2 and Cover 3 are the zones you will see most frequently, there are lots of other coverage strategies. In Quarters coverage, to guard against the deep pass, the defensive backs each cover one-fourth of the field. On the other hand, a defense might play straight man-to-man, usually when they send a big blitz. Man-to-man defense is only effective if the rushers get to the quarterback very quickly. To give some protection against the deep pass in man-to-man coverage, one safety could play deep while everyone else covers a man. This is called Cover 1.

The Specialists: Kickers, Punters, and Blocking the Kick

You might think that the kicking team would be considered part of the offense. Perhaps it should be, as they are trying to score points. However, the kicking unit, as well as the players who return kicks, are considered separate from both offense and defense. Kick and kick return units are called the special teams. Usually, especially in college and the NFL, players on the special teams are not starters on offense or defense. These units have special, separate practice times. Watch a game closely. When it's time for a punt or a field goal, you'll see mass substitutions as the special teams run onto the field.

The Importance of Special Teams

Some coaches tell their teams that the punt is the most important play in football. Think of how much yardage is traded in just a single punt—nearly half the field! Think about how big a deal it is for a team to block a punt or to return one for a touchdown. That can change a game.

TOUCHBACK: If the kickoff goes into the end zone, the offense gets the ball at the 20- or 25-yard line. If the ball doesn't go into the end zone, the kick returner can sometimes get farther than that.

COFFIN CORNER: The best possible punt will go out of bounds but will not get into the end zone for a touchback. Punters often practice aiming their punts so they'll go out of bounds inside the 5-yard line. Such a punt is called a coffin corner punt.

The Kickoff

On a kickoff, the kicking team not only have to kick the ball way down the field; they also have to tackle anyone who tries to return the kick. The techniques used by members of the kicking team are similar to those of a defense: Avoid blocks, get in position, and make a tackle. Positioning is even more important on a kickoff than on a regular play because the players are so spread out. A kick returner who catches the ball can usually run 10–15 yards before coming anywhere near a tackler. The tacklers have to run very fast and stay away from blockers until they get near the returner. Then they have to position themselves so the returner can't get away. A tackle on a kickoff usually isn't made by one person flying full speed in the open field. It's usually made by a whole bunch of tacklers closing in until they can make the play together.

Good kickoffs go high, deep, and toward one side of the field. The higher the kick, the longer the kicking team has to run down the field to get in the right position. By kicking to one side, the kicking team reduces the amount of field they have to cover. But the kicker has to be careful. If the kick goes out of bounds, the return team gets the ball at the 40-yard line.

As the kicking team tries to tackle the kick returner, the members of the return team are trying to block for the returner. Positioning is very important on a kick return. A blocker tries to get in between the defender and the returner to push the defender away. That's harder than it sounds because the defenders are all running as fast as they can. It's unlikely that a blocker will knock anyone down; but they'll try to push, shove, and use their hands to make the defender go the wrong way.

The Punt

The kicking, tackling, and return strategies for punts are similar to those on kickoffs. There are a few main differences:

- Before the punting team runs downfield, they have to block to protect the punter. Their most important job is to prevent the punt from being blocked. Only after the punt is kicked should the team race to tackle the returner.
- If a punt goes out of bounds, the receiving team gets the ball right where it left the field. So it's usually a good idea to boom a punt out of bounds—then no one can return it!
- The gunners. Usually the punting team lines up two fast players near the sidelines. These are the gunners, who don't bother protecting the punter. At the snap, the gunners race downfield toward the potential returner as if they were in kickoff coverage. Problem is, the return team is allowed to line up right across from the gunners. The gunners have to find a way around one or two players who are trying to bump, push, and hit them. Try watching the gunners next time you see a punt to see the kinds of moves they make to get themselves down the field.

Field Goals and Extra Points

If all goes right, a field goal or an extra point should be routine. The long snapper gets the ball to the holder, who puts the ball down for the kicker to kick. The only reason these plays look easy is that teams practice them over and over and over.

The Long Snapper

On many teams, the long snapper is not the regular center. The long snapper's primary job is to snap the football back quickly and accurately to the holder, then to block. But blocking is far less important than the accuracy of the snap. The long snapper practices snaps for hours each week. In fact, there are special summer camps dedicated just to

FUN FACT

Shane Lechler's Powerful Leg

Shane Lechler punted for eighteen years in the NFL. He began his career with Oakland in 2000, where he won a Super Bowl. Over his career, Lechler averaged better than 47 yards per punt—an NFL career record. He retired after the 2017 season when he averaged 49 yards per punt!

Illegal Blocks

It seems like a whole lot of kick returns result in penalties for illegal blocks. Kick return blockers cannot block below the waist or in the back. If they do, the penalty is 10 yards from the spot of the illegal block. Therefore, it's better just to let someone make a tackle than to make an illegal block on him.

Wacky Weather

Use a dark marker to color in all the squares with the letters H-O-T. When you are finished, you will have the silly answer to the riddle.

Why did the stadium get hot after the game?

P	D	H	O	T	L	H	L	Y	T	E	B	P	I
I	E	O	G	H	K	O	P	J	O	W	R	E	K
U	Q	T	H	O	U	T	G	K	H	A	E	W	J
Y	A	H	J	T	I	H	M	L	O	Q	B	Q	L
R	S	O	K	H	I	T	H	A	T	O	H	A	P
E	Z	G	L	K	Y	P	D	S	J	M	P	S	Y
W	X	H	H	O	P	T	E	H	K	H	O	X	B
Q	C	A	O	J	R	O	Y	O	L	O	D	Z	N
A	V	C	T	K	E	H	H	T	P	T	H	D	M
S	B	V	H	A	W	T	K	T	V	O	P	F	Z
D	N	F	T	S	S	O	L	O	C	H	O	C	A
E	M	E	G	W	D	K	M	F	X	D	G	V	S
H	O	N	H	H	H	J	H	G	Z	T	R	O	H
O	U	J	T	M	O	W	O	H	A	T	E	H	R
T	H	K	O	H	T	S	T	L	O	O	W	T	T
T	K	M	O	J	H	D	T	P	G	H	S	J	O
H	M	L	H	P	O	R	O	R	N	O	F	O	H
K	L	R	F	R	K	F	Y	E	M	A	R	G	D
O	P	Y	H	O	L	O	H	S	H	H	O	F	H
H	J	P	T	J	Y	H	D	W	J	O	M	D	O
O	K	W	O	T	R	T	O	A	S	T	N	E	T
T	I	E	H	L	E	T	G	Z	W	O	B	R	Y
H	T	Q	O	H	D	O	L	X	Y	O	X	Q	O

long-snapping skills! Fans rarely see the name of the long snappers, but they're the next most important players on special teams behind the punters or kickers. If a kick goes bad, it's probably because of a less-than-perfect snap.

The Holder

The holder is usually also a team's backup quarterback or punter. He stoops on one knee, ready to catch the snap and place the ball on the ground. Ideally, he puts the ball straight up and down, with the laces pointing away from the kicker.

The Kicker

Years ago, kickers ran straight up to the ball and kicked it with their toe. In the 1970s, kickers figured out that the ball goes farther if it's kicked from the side, like a soccer player kicks. This kicking technique was called soccer style. Good high school kickers can consistently kick the ball through the uprights from at least 30 to 35 yards. In college and in the pros, kickers have to be accurate from much farther away. In fact, NFL kickers routinely hit 50-yard field goals.

You might have practiced kicking before. If you used a kicking tee and if you approached the ball at a full sprint, you might have been able to kick the ball a long way, maybe even 30 or more yards. So you can kick field goals for a college team, right? Well, you weren't really kicking a field goal. Kicking tees are only allowed for kickoffs, and NFL kickers can kick the ball 60–80 yards on a kickoff. For a field goal, the ball must be held on the ground. Making it even more difficult, the kicker has to kick a field goal quickly, before the defense can rush in to block it. The kicker actually starts the run-up to the kick before the holder is holding the ball! On a kickoff, the kicker might run 10–15 yards on his run-up, but he only gets 5–7 yards for a field goal.

The Bills and Ace Ventura

In Super Bowl XXV, Bills kicker Scott Norwood missed a field goal wide right that would have won the game. On that kick, the holder put the laces the wrong way. In the movie *Ace Ventura: Pet Detective*, one of the characters is a kicker who, like Norwood, missed an important kick partially because the holder held the ball wrong.

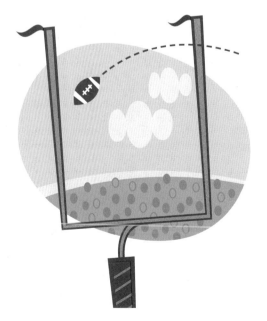

Super Fans

Football GREAT

Travis Kelce

This Ohio native was drafted by the Kansas City Chiefs from the University of Cincinnati in 2013. Since then, he has been regarded as the best tight end in football. Not only can he block; his receiving stats are better than those of many wide receivers. He's had seven 1,000-yard receiving seasons, and he scores touchdowns, four of them in the double digits. And he has consistently performed well, with 800–1,400 yards in every single season since 2014. Put a tight end who scores like a wide receiver on your fantasy team if you can!

WORDS TO KNOW

COMMISSIONER: The commissioner is like the referee of fantasy football, someone who keeps the game running. This person keeps track of statistics (which usually just means keeping an eye on the website that does your stats for you), sets up the rules of the league and the draft, and makes the final decisions if there are disagreements.

Fantasy Leagues

Imagine owning a football team. You're the person in charge of everything, from the uniform design to player moves to game strategy. Wouldn't that be great? There's no reason you can't own an NFL franchise someday. All it costs to own a team is several thousand million dollars. What? You don't think you'll have a billion dollars to spare anytime soon? Then the closest substitute for you will be to own a fantasy football team.

The Basics of Fantasy Football

Each fantasy league has different rules, but they have the same basic idea. You'll choose a number of NFL players to be on your team. Every time one of your players does something good—scores a touchdown, gains yards, kicks a field goal—your team gains points. If your player does something bad, though, like throwing an interception or losing a fumble, your team loses points.

Each weekend your team will play against another team in your league. You'll play one player, or sometimes two players, at each position, and so will your opponent. Add up all the points your players score over their games that weekend. If you score more points than your opponent, you win your fantasy game.

How the League Works

Each week you set your lineup, which means you pick one or two players at each position to represent your team. You have to pick carefully. If one of your players scores three touchdowns in his NFL game that week and you left him on the bench, you'll feel silly.

Once the NFL games start on Sunday afternoon, you can sit back and watch. Now that you're playing fantasy football, you are doing more than rooting for your favorite NFL team. You're also rooting for all of your players to do well. That means you have a special interest in more than just one game.

Fantasy Draft Strategies

During the draft, you will be under pressure to make very quick decisions about which players to choose. If you've made a list ahead of time of which players are best, you'll have an easier time during the actual draft.

There are several ways to make your list. One thought is to rank the top two hundred or so players in the order you'd want them. Then when it's your turn to pick, you will lean toward taking the highest-ranking player left. This sort of list will help the most in the early rounds when you still need to fill pretty much every position on your roster. Another idea is to make several shorter lists, ranking the top thirty or so players at each position. This sort of list can help the most in later rounds when you need to fill specific positions.

In some leagues it might not be easy to get the owners together for a draft. In that case, the league can let the computer pick everyone's team. All owners submit a list of players ranked in the order they'd like to choose them. The computer goes from team to team, letting each team have the highest-ranked player remaining on their list. Automatic drafts are less fun and they allow for less strategy, but they're quite a lot quicker than live drafts.

Choosing Your Starters

The roster will usually have more than one player for each position. If your league lets you start one quarterback each week, then you'll probably have an extra quarterback on the bench. That way, if your star quarterback gets hurt or if he's not

Where to Get Help with Your List

Each summer, you can find many fantasy football magazines and websites that provide lists of players like the ones you'll need for your draft. It is easiest to start with a list made by someone else and then change it around to suit your needs.

TRY THIS

Customize Your League's Scoring

The standard scoring system for most fantasy leagues awards 6 points for a touchdown and 1 point for every 10 yards gained. Quarterbacks might get 1 point for every 25 passing yards. Kickers usually get 1 point for an extra point and 3 or more for a field goal. Defenses usually earn points for turnovers and touchdowns, with bonuses for yardage and points allowed. But you and your league's commissioner can set up your scoring system however you like.

Football GREAT

Sam Kerr

Sam Kerr grew up near Perth, Australia. She played Australian rules football, which is a very rough version of tackle football played without helmets and pads. Because her area didn't have girls' teams, she played with boys until she was twelve years old. And she was a standout player. After that, she switched to playing soccer. Today, she is one of the best female soccer players in the world…but she started as a football player!

doing well, you can replace him with your extra quarterback. The same reasoning applies to the other positions as well.

Each week you declare which of your players are starting; that is, which statistics will count toward your league for that week's games. You can only start some of your players, with the rest sitting out for the week.

Sometimes the decision of who to start is pretty obvious. If you have, say, Patrick Mahomes and Gardner Minshew at quarterback, you're going to start Mahomes, the guy who's been one of the top-scoring quarterbacks since he entered the NFL. On the other hand, if Mahomes's Chiefs are on their bye week and not playing, then you'll have to start Minshew.

Other times, it isn't clear who you should start. Imagine you have two wide receivers. One is playing against the best pass defense in the NFL, and the other is playing against one of the worst defensive teams. Who should you start? In general, you should always play a true star, someone like Davante Adams or Tyreek Hill. Beyond the All-Pro players, it's often a good idea to start the player whose team plays against the really bad defense.

NFL Injury Words

You certainly don't want to start someone who turns out to be injured. Be sure to read the NFL injury reports before making your decision. The official NFL injury reports are issued the Friday before a Sunday game. A player will be described with one of three words:

- *Questionable* means it's uncertain if a player will play.
- *Doubtful* means it's unlikely a player will play.
- *Out* means the player will not play.

You'll discover that teams use these descriptions differently and sometimes unpredictably. It hurts your fantasy team a lot if you start a quarterback who was listed as questionable only to see him sit on the bench. But there's nothing you can do then. The best strategy you can use is to sit anyone who's doubtful and don't start a questionable player unless you read in a couple of news articles that he's likely to play.

How to Find Out More

If you didn't watch a game, a box score can help you figure out what happened and how your favorite players did. If you own a fantasy football team, the box score gives you the information you need to calculate how many points your players scored.

Print newspapers love box scores because they can tell you so much about a game, yet they don't take much space to print. The paper can put all of a day's box scores on half a page, and you'll know what happened in yesterday's games, as well as how all of your players did.

But what if you want to find out more about a game? Ask a parent if you can go online to www.nfl.com. Find the "scores" page. An hour or so after a game is completed, you can click on a game to see more details and to watch highlights. Click on "Download Game Book" at the bottom of the page. You'll see everyone who played, a summary of every play (including who made each tackle), drive charts, and even more statistics than are in the box score.

The Pro Football Hall of Fame

If you're a fan of the NFL, you will love a trip to the Hall of Fame in Canton, Ohio. Even though the players and teams that you'll see there probably played before you started following football, you'll still enjoy learning some of the football history you've heard about.

Draft Advice

Kickers are the least important position in fantasy football. Sure, some kickers are better than others, but you can always find a starting kicker on the waiver wire who can do nearly as well as the best kicker in the league. Don't draft a kicker until the last round! Use your valuable draft picks on the offensive skill positions first.

YAC: *YAC* stands for "yards after catch." If a receiver catches the ball 10 yards from the line of scrimmage and then runs another 20 yards, that's considered to be a 30-yard pass! A fast receiver might gain a lot of his yards after he catches the ball.

BOX SCORE: A newspaper or website will print a summary of a game and its statistics, called a box score, where you can tell how many yards players gained rushing, receiving, and passing and how each team scored their points.

Backfield Buzz

Put the football vocab words in the grid in alphabetical order from top to bottom. When you are finished, read down the shaded column to get the answer to the riddle.

Which insect has the hardest time playing football?

OUT OF BOUNDS

LATERAL

HALFBACK

DEFENSE

CARRY

PENALTY

REFEREE

FOUL

HOLDING

GAME BALL

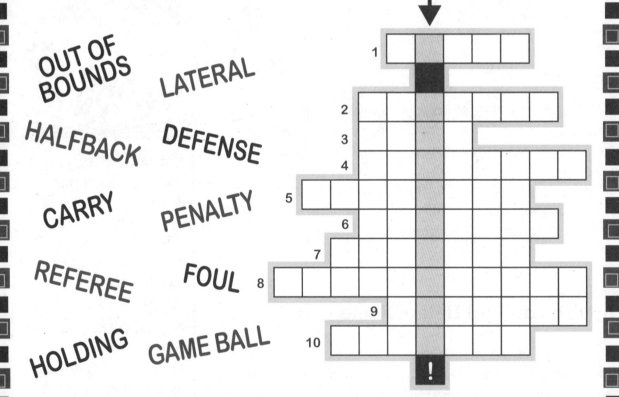

What's in There?

When you enter the building, you'll see an enormous room with a domed roof. In the middle is a life-sized statue of Jim Thorpe, one of the first true football stars.

In the galleries around the statue are some of the Hall's most historically interesting displays, including:

- The shoe used to kick the longest field goal ever
- Jim Brown's helmet
- Walter Payton's game uniform from when he broke the all-time rushing record
- Y.A. Tittle's old-style helmet that was cracked in half during a game
- An enormous knee brace worn by Joe Namath

The other members of the Hall of Fame don't get full life-sized statues, but they do all get bronze busts of their heads. One large room contains all of these busts. The Hall contains displays celebrating great players of the past and present. These displays may show a game uniform, a photo of a player in action, or a plaque summarizing his accomplishments. Many of the player displays are grouped by team.

The Hall has a display of equipment worn by football players throughout history. You'll be amazed at the leather helmets without facemasks, the old-style shoulder pads, and the strange-looking balls that were used in the 1920s. There are the actual jerseys worn by players when important events happened. For example, you can see the uniform LaDainian Tomlinson wore when he set the NFL's single-season touchdown record in 2006. The Hall collects footballs used in historic games and stores them in a huge room in boxes on shelves.

It can be confusing to be a fan of fantasy football. Fill in the blanks to see one reason why. There are three possible letters you can use in each blank. Be careful — we've given you one extra fantasy letter.

Im __ gine t __ __ t

__ f __ nt __ sy

o __ ner __ __ s pl __ yers

from t __ o

different te __ ms.

__ __ en bot __ "re __ l"

te __ ms pl __ y e __ ch

ot __ er, t __ e

f __ nt __ sy o __ ner

__ ill __ ope t __ __ t

bot __ te __ ms

score __ lot!

Fans Have Fun

Football fans really get into cheering on the team! Can you find your way from START to END through the crazy crowd?

Women in the Hall of Fame

The Hall of Fame exhibit called "Women's Impact on Football" includes commemorative items honoring female coaches, referees, and Women's Football Alliance players. The headsets worn by Andrea Kremer and Hannah Storm—the first all-female NFL broadcast crew—are there!

How Are the Hall of Fame Players Chosen?

Hall of Fame players are chosen by a selection committee. There's usually one representative for each city with an NFL team in it—with two for New York since they have two teams—and sixteen other selectors who can come from anywhere. The selectors are usually members of the media who have followed their team for a while and know a lot about football.

On the day before the Super Bowl, the whole committee meets to talk about that year's candidates. One person presents an argument for each. Once the discussion is over, the selectors vote. The players with the most support become members of the Hall of Fame. Each year, the selectors can't choose more than eight.

The ceremony that makes someone a member happens in July in Canton. Players are shown their busts, they're given gold jackets, and they make speeches.

CHAPTER 9

Behind the Scenes

The Bosses on the Practice Field: The Coaching Staff

The head coach, especially the head coach of a major college or NFL team, is hardly behind the scenes. In fact, many big-time head coaches host a weekly television show! Even high school head coaches are well known in their communities. The assistant coaches and the coaches of the lower-level high school teams, though, are not household names. These folks work hard too, but not many people (aside from the players and school community) are likely to know who they are or what they do.

College and Professional Assistant Coaches

Assistant coaches at the college and NFL level are career coaches, for the most part. They have decided that they want to learn how to be a big-time coach, often (but not always) with the goal of becoming a head coach somewhere. Coaching is these folks' full-time job. Most assistants are position coaches, with one person in charge of linebackers, another for defensive backs, and so on. An assistant's role is to relate personally to each player they are in charge of and to help those players develop their skills. In season, assistant coaches must understand each game plan and then figure out how to teach their players to execute that plan. If an effective football team consists of lots of different units working together, then the assistant coaches are the ones who train each individual unit.

High School Assistant Coaches

At the high school level, most assistants are teachers at the school. At first, you may think it a bit strange to have teachers as football coaches, especially if they teach something like physics or art. It's not these teachers' academic knowledge that is useful on the football field as much as their teaching ability. Coaching, after all, is teaching: explaining techniques, motivating, helping players learn new and sometimes difficult approaches. Coaching is not a high school assistant's full-time job. But then football is not a high school player's full-time job either. The players often develop an improved appreciation for their coaches' classes. They may not have enjoyed chemistry class before, but if the offensive line coach is also the chemistry teacher, they might find the subject more manageable.

Who Makes You Look Good: The Equipment Manager

The equipment manager is one of the most important parts of the support staff during the game. If someone's helmet breaks, they simply can't play unless someone, usually the equipment manager, fixes it. The equipment manager is also in charge of making sure every player's uniform is ready to go on game day.

Uniforms

Football is an all-weather outdoor sport. After a game, those great-looking uniforms become covered with grass stains, mud, and sweat. The equipment manager's main job is to get the uniforms clean for the next game. That's not an easy task considering the average team has seventy to a hundred sets of jerseys, pants, socks, and so on. Holes in jerseys have to be sewn back together. The uniforms go through the wash seven or eight times and are treated in between to help remove stains. When they're finally done, each complete uniform is assembled and hung in the correct player's locker. And there's more... much, much more. So much more, in fact, that a major college or NFL program has as many as ten to twenty people working under the supervision of the head equipment manager.

While the laundry from last week's game is in the machines, the equipment managers get ready for the week's practices. Each team's specific routine is different, but the main idea is the same for all: get each player the correct practice jersey. This is more complicated than you might think. The team can't all look the same for practice because they have to have different-colored jerseys for offense and defense. Some teams have even more different outfits. Perhaps the starters and reserves wear different colors too. The coaches might also have special requests. For example, if the next opponent wears green and has a really good linebacker who wears the number 50, the coaches might ask for one of their own scout team linebackers to wear a green number-50 jersey in practice. The equipment managers have to sort out the practice jerseys, giving the correct one to each player; then they have to have all the rest of the players' equipment ready, including helmets, pads, and shoes.

Heavy Lifting

While laundry and practice preparation are going on, the staff is still unpacking stuff from the previous week's game, cleaning, organizing, and repacking for the next week's game. During a game, things get damaged, broken, and lost. The equipment manager must be able to replace any piece of equipment instantly. That takes organization and planning. The team brings extra shoes, cleats, pants, mouthpieces, pads, and pretty much anything needed to keep every player properly outfitted and available for the whole game. It takes a good part of a week's work to get all of this spare stuff in the right place, ready for travel to the game site.

Two or three days before an away game, the entire staff loads everything onto a huge truck. This truck drives to the game, arriving well before the team. The equipment managers themselves fly with the team, but they don't get to go right

FUN FACT

Equipment Staff Rituals

At Penn State University, the head equipment manager and staff spend every Thursday night before a game repairing and painting the players' black shoes. Then they clean and repair the players' white helmets. At Notre Dame, before each game, the helmets receive a fresh coat of gold paint. Almost every equipment staff has some kind of special pregame custom. Do you know the staff ritual of your favorite team?

Fancy Footwork

Solve the letter and number equations to find the answer to the riddle.

Why did the official kick Cinderella out of the game?

A + 4
I - 1
P + 3
X + 1
G - 2
I + 4
B - 1
F + 2
R + 1
T + 3
V - 2
V - 1
D - 3
D - 3
J + 3
J + 2
A + 2
M + 1
L + 3
N - 2
G - 2
E - 4
S - 1
D - 3
G - 5
P + 2
D + 2
A + 1

FWEEET!!

to the team hotel. They have to meet the truck and unload all of the equipment onto the sideline before they can rest.

The head equipment manager can work eighty-hour weeks during the season. That's crazy—forty hours per week is the standard for most workers! Taking care of a team's stuff is long, hard work, but it all pays off on game day.

All-Around Helper: The Team Manager

Think about all the small jobs that need to be done to help out a football team. There are a lot of these. Someone needs to fill up water bottles before practice and during practice, then the water bottles need to be cleaned up and put away. What about the footballs themselves? Someone has to take charge of giving out footballs to various coaches and players who need them for practice, then collecting them after practice, finding any that got thrown into the bushes, and putting them away where they belong.

Managers are critical to the team's success, so a good coaching staff will bend over backward to let them know their importance. Managers pack up for away games with the rest of the equipment staff. They prowl the sideline on game day, filling whatever role is needed. Some will fetch and (on bad-weather days) clean the game balls.

OW!: The Athletic Trainer

Football is a hard-hitting game. After a game or a hard practice, every player, even the best-conditioned athlete, feels sore. Isn't it great that the athletic trainer is there, waiting to help you feel better?

TRY THIS

Respecting the Student Managers

Unfortunately, sometimes there are players who don't understand how important and hardworking the managers are. A good coach will not allow disrespectful behavior. Most coaches lecture the team at the beginning of the season about how to treat the managers respectfully. At the end of the year, the coaches make sure that the managers get the same kind of honors as the players do.

The Athletic Trainer's Job

Most high school athletic programs have an athletic trainer who works with athletes in all their sports. Colleges and NFL football teams employ four or five trainers for their roster of sixty to ninety players. These trainers are all an integral part of the team. During the seven months of the season, these dedicated folks work seven days a week. They tape ankles and otherwise prepare every player for every practice. They help supervise rehabilitation. After practice, trainers help players ice, stretch, and otherwise assist their bodies to start the recovery process so they'll be ready for the next practice.

Major injuries in football are, in fact, reasonably rare. Studies show that soccer players are considerably more likely to suffer serious injuries than football players. Why? One of many reasons for the low injury rate is that football teams actively work to prevent injury. The athletic trainers supervise the stretching and taping that is an important part of injury prevention. Trainers also attend daily to all the nagging minor soreness and strains that could become major injuries without treatment. And, of course, state-of-the-art protective equipment absorbs most of the hard hits.

NFL athletic trainers travel with the team the day before a game. At the team hotel, the training staff takes over a big conference room to use as a training room. On game day, the athletic trainers work nonstop. They open up their hotel training room as early as they wake up. Then they move all of their equipment to the game site. Several hours before the game, players begin to show up for pregame preparation. The trainers will spend at least five minutes (or much more!) per player taping ankles, stretching out tight muscles, covering protective casts, and making sure that every player's body is ready by game time.

During the game, the athletic trainers spread out on the sideline with the team. They are instantly ready to deal with injuries, both major and minor. They (along with the team doctor) tell the coach which injured players can get back in the game and who needs to sit out. Game time is what the athletic trainers live for. Even though they're not playing, they get the same rush of excitement as the players do because seventy thousand fans are screaming for the team to win, and the athletic trainers are part of that team.

The athletic trainer's job never ends. Even on the plane ride home, athletic trainers are giving out ice packs and making sure injured players are positioned correctly. Then, after everyone else has gone home, they stick around for an extra hour or so with injured players to get treatment started right away.

Keeping a Clean Game: The Officials

There is a job you can do every weekend. You'll have to spend hours ahead of time getting ready: going to meetings, studying, and traveling. You have to pass a test to be allowed to do the job. When it's time to start, you'll be expected to sprint a total of several miles to keep up with people who are faster than you. You can expect to get knocked down occasionally by giants wearing armor. Everyone—maybe thousands of people—will complain about everything you do. They'll scream at you and call you names, even if you do a good job. When it's all over, you'll get paid. Woo-hoo! Go to the bookstore to spend your paycheck, and you'll be able to buy maybe two books. Such is the life of a football official.

Though they do hard work, football officials truly love what they are doing. For one thing, they know how critical they are to the game. Can you imagine a game without officials? That wouldn't work. Though fans and coaches will yell

Loads of Laundry

Jonas _____

Tom _____

Jean _____

Lonny _____

Lida _____

There are 48 jerseys to wash and repair before the next game. Figure out how many jerseys each of the five equipment managers is responsible for.

- Jonas gets 13 jerseys
- Tom gets twice as many jerseys as Jean
- Jean gets as many jerseys as Lonny
- Lida gets 10 fewer jerseys than Jonas
  Jean gets 5 jerseys more than Lida

at them, most of them respect the tremendous effort that officials put into calling every game.

The people who officiate do so for many reasons. Many are former athletes who are too old to play anymore but who still love football and want to stay involved. Some might not have been good enough to play football but are extremely good at calling the game. Officials must be just as focused in their minds and their bodies as the players are during a game.

There are a fair number of female officials throughout the country as well. In 2015, after a long and successful NCAA career, Sarah Thomas joined an NFL officiating crew as a line judge. She worked her first playoff game in 2019 and worked the Super Bowl as a down judge in 2021. In fact, the officiating position called "down judge" was until a few years ago called the "head linesman." The position was renamed because of Sarah Thomas. She was a female head "linesman," which didn't make sense to anyone. So the NFL made the position name gender neutral!

Most importantly, despite the craziness, officiating football can be fun. How many times have you watched a game on TV and wished you could be part of the action?

Officiating Positions

Football officials work in teams. A junior varsity game might have four officials. The NFL and most college conferences use seven officials on a team. Every member of the team has a different job to do:

- The **referee** is the crew chief, supervising all the officials on the team. During the game, the referee stands behind the offense and is primarily responsible for watching the quarterback. The referee announces penalties to the coaches and the spectators.
- The **umpire** stands directly behind the defensive line. Their job is to watch the blockers to make sure no one is holding. The umpire also gets the ball ready for the next play.
- The **down judge** and the line judge stand on the sideline, right on the line of scrimmage. They both look to see that the play starts correctly, and then they are responsible for any action near the sideline. The down judge runs the chain crew, making sure they can measure for a first down if necessary.
- The **field judge**, **side judge**, and **back judge** start each play way behind the defense. They watch out for pass interference. They take over watching the action when a play goes for long yardage. Some leagues, especially in high school, only use a field judge, not a side or back judge.

Women Can Be Players Too

There is no rule anywhere that girls can't play football on boys' teams, but it's very rare to see a female player on a high school team, usually because boys simply grow bigger and stronger. In 2020, Sarah Fuller became the first woman to play NCAA football when she kicked for Vanderbilt. In 2023, Haley Van Voorhis became the first non-kicker college player as a safety for Shenandoah University.

White Hat

Officials other than the referee wear black hats with teeny white stripes. The referee, though, wears a pure white hat. Among officials, the term *white hat* refers to the referee.

The Statisticians Know More Than Just the Score

Have you ever heard a television broadcaster say something like "That reception gives Julio Jones 300 receiving yards today, only the sixth time in NFL history that has happened"? Well, it's not like the announcer added up Jones's yards in his head. At every football game, from the high school level to the NFL, one or more statisticians are keeping track of what happens on every play. These folks are the ones who know all the important numbers behind the game.

Statisticians at High School Games

A high school team usually asks a student, or perhaps a parent, to volunteer to keep statistics during its games. This person works either on the sideline or in the press box, writing down who carried or passed the ball and how many yards he gained on each play. They also write down how each team scored touchdowns or field goals. At the end of the game, the statistician writes a box score; usually, this box score is then sent to a local newspaper to be published the next day.

After each game, the statistician also puts together the team's overall season stats. These are used at the end of the season to help decide who gets team or all-state awards.

Statisticians at College and NFL Games

There are so many football statistics that people like to know about. It's not hard for one volunteer to collect rushing and passing yardage. But other stuff is harder to keep track of. How many times did the team make it on third down? How many tackles did each defender make? How many penalties did the team commit, and how many yards did they cost? Some of these things can be figured out by scouts, by watching video of the game. But at the college and NFL level, fans want to know these things immediately as they watch

Stats Perform

Stats Perform, formerly known as STATS, LCC, is a company that hires reporters to watch every college and NFL game to keep statistics. On game day, Stats Perform provides live score updates to websites and television stations. Even video game programmers use the information collected by Stats Perform to help make their games realistic.

them on television. So, a lot of people work together to put together all of the stats.

Several people might be assigned to look at different parts of each play—one person for offense, one for defense, for example. Computers store the data and do all the math so that people can see results right away. In the press box, screens are updated after each play with information from the statisticians. A television announcer can just look at this screen to see live stats.

The Scouts

Teams need to know about the team they're playing next. What kind of offense and defense do they run? Who are their best players? The strategies a team uses will depend on what they think the other team will do. Figuring out what the other team can do is called scouting.

In high school, scouting is usually done by just a few coaches watching video. College and NFL coaches also watch video of their opponents...but the higher the level of football, the more intense the scouting that goes on. Imagine that the NFL team that you coach is playing the Ravens next week. How do you get your game plan ready?

You'll use a whole lot of people to figure out how the Ravens play. First of all, you'll send people to this week's Ravens game. These folks will sit in the press box or the stands, making notes on what they see. How many seconds does it take for the punter to kick the ball? How far away does the field goal kicker make his warm-up kicks? How is Lamar Jackson talking to his receivers on the sideline? Which coach seems to be sending in the defensive plays? Any of these things might give you an idea to help you win next week.

FUN FACT

Pro Football Reference

Perhaps the most comprehensive site for NFL statistics is www.profootball-reference.com. Click on a game from this season or any season since 1920(!). You'll get a box score, starters, a complete play-by-play of the game, and even a chart estimating the chances of each team winning after each play. You can find single-season and all-time records in any category you might imagine. This is the site for a football stats enthusiast to get lost in.

WORDS TO KNOW

PLAY ACTION: A fake handoff to a running back before a quarterback tries to throw a pass is called *play action*.

Next, you'll look at what the statisticians say about the Ravens. These statisticians will record all kinds of details about every Ravens play in every game, this year and in years past. How many defensive players lined up on the line of scrimmage? Which cornerback covered the strongest receiver? How often did they run play action? Maybe you can figure out a tip that might help you know whether a play is a running or a passing play, or what route a receiver will run.

And finally, you'll watch video, just like a high school coach. In the NFL, though, a staff of video coordinators will have used computer editing equipment to make video watching easier. Do you want to see all of the Ravens running plays to the right side on third down? Click a button. Would you rather see every play when Jackson threw a long pass? Just click. You can quickly see whatever kind of play you want.

So you see, while a game is played by only twenty-two players at a time, and for three or so hours once a week, lots and lots of people are working all week to make sure the game goes well. And each week, thousands of games are played, in high school, college, and the NFL. Is it any wonder that football is the most-loved sport in America?

Watching "Film"?

Way back before your parents were born, the only way to see a recording of another team's game was to watch film projected like in a movie theater. Nowadays, coaches usually watch video on a computer.

APPENDIX A Football Facts and Records

The records football players hold help fans understand just how good they were. Here are some of the important NFL individual career records as of the end of the 2023 season:

Most NFL Rushing Yards

Emmitt Smith	Cowboys, Cardinals	18,355
Walter Payton	Bears	16,726
Frank Gore	49ers, Colts, Dolphins, Bills	16,000
Barry Sanders	Lions	15,269

Most Passing Yards

Tom Brady	Patriots, Buccaneers	89,214
Drew Brees	Chargers, Saints	80,358
Peyton Manning	Colts, Broncos	71,940

Most Receiving Yards

Jerry Rice	49ers, Raiders, Seahawks	22,895
Larry Fitzgerald	Cardinals	17,492
Terrell Owens	49ers, Eagles, Cowboys, and others	15,934

Most Touchdowns Scored

Jerry Rice	49ers, Raiders, Seahawks	208
Emmitt Smith	Cowboys, Cardinals	175
LaDainian Tomlinson	Chargers, Jets	162

Most Points Scored

Adam Vinatieri	Patriots, Colts	2,673
Morten Andersen	Saints, Falcons, and others	2,544
Gary Anderson	Steelers, Vikings, and others	2,434

NFL Team Records

While individuals are important, football is a team game. Here are some NFL team records:

Most Super Bowl Victories

Steelers, Patriots	6
Cowboys, 49ers	5

Most NFL Championships

Packers	13
Bears	9
Giants	8

Most Super Bowls Played

Patriots	11
Cowboys, Steelers, Broncos, 49ers	8
Chiefs	6

College Team Records

It's tough to find meaningful college football records. Since there wasn't a multiteam playoff until 2014, each year might have several national champions. Individual statistics don't mean a lot either, since some teams schedule easy games to get players more yards gained. But here are some notable records:

Most National Championships since 1936

Alabama	13
Notre Dame	9
Ohio State	8

Most SEC Championships

Alabama	30
Georgia	14
Tennessee	13

Most Big Ten Championships

Michigan	45
Ohio State	39
Minnesota	18

Most Rose Bowl Victories

Southern California	25
Michigan, Ohio State	8

The Heisman Trophy

The Heisman is awarded each year to an outstanding college football player. Football writers and broadcasters vote for the winner.

Most Heisman Trophies

Archie Griffin	Ohio State	2

Heisman Trophy winners who are playing in the NFL as of the 2023 season include:

- Joe Burrow, LSU—quarterback for the Bengals
- Kyler Murray, Oklahoma—quarterback for the Cardinals
- Baker Mayfield, Oklahoma—quarterback for the Buccaneers
- Lamar Jackson, Louisville—quarterback for the Ravens
- Derrick Henry, Alabama—running back for the Titans
- Marcus Mariota, Oregon—quarterback for the Eagles
- Jameis Winston, Florida State—quarterback for the Saints
- Bryce Young, Alabama—quarterback for the Panthers
- DaVonta Smith, Alabama—wide receiver for the Eagles

APPENDIX B Glossary

Athletic scholarship:
Money given to a college athlete to pay for tuition and living expenses.

Ball security:
Holding on to the ball correctly so as not to fumble.

Blitz:
When more than four defensive players rush the quarterback.

Box score:
A summary of a game and its statistics printed in a newspaper or on a website.

Bye:
A week when a team doesn't play a game. NFL teams get one bye each season.

Chain gang:
The people who carry a chain to indicate the line for the next first down.

Coffin corner:
A punt that goes out of bounds near (but not in) the end zone.

Commissioner:
The person in charge of a league. The commissioner of the NFL is Roger Goodell. A fantasy league also appoints a commissioner.

Contain:
The defensive line tries to keep, or contain, the quarterback in the pocket.

Crossing routes:
When receivers run routes with crossing paths, designed to confuse a zone defense.

Defense:
The part of a football team that tries to stop the offense from scoring.

Down:
The offense gets four plays to gain at least ten yards. These four plays are called *downs*.

Draw play:
A running play that starts after the defense thinks it's a passing play.

Dump-off:
A short pass designed to fool the defense.

Eligible receiver:
Anyone who is allowed to catch a pass. This usually includes everyone except the five offensive linemen.

Flea flicker:
A trick play. The running back is handed the ball and starts to run but throws the ball back to the quarterback who throws a long pass to a receiver.

Fumble:
When a runner drops the ball, that's a fumble—either team can pick up the ball.

Holding:
Unless he's trying to tackle the ball-carrier, no one is allowed to grab, hug, or tackle. Holding results in a 10-yard penalty.

Homecoming:
The game when the school's graduates come back to watch and celebrate.

Home-field advantage:
For a lot of reasons, the home team wins about 60 percent of all NFL games.

Hot receiver:
A receiver who runs a very short route, called a hot route. The receiver is ready to catch the ball right away so the quarterback can avoid being sacked during a blitz.

Hot route:
A route run by a receiver for when the defense blitzes.

Independents:
College football teams that do not belong to a conference.

Interception:
When the defensive team catches a pass that the offensive team threw.

Lateral:
A backward pass. Any player can throw a lateral at any time.

APPENDIX B: GLOSSARY

Line of scrimmage:
Where the referee places the ball at the beginning of a play. Neither the offense nor the defense is allowed to cross the line.

Merger, the:
In 1970, the American Football League and the National Football League came together to form a single NFL.

NIL (Name, Image, or Likeness):
Since many college players are famous, they may accept money for their name, image, or likeness to appear in ads.

NFL:
These initials stand for National Football League. This is the most successful professional sports league in the world.

Offense:
The part of a football team that controls the ball and tries to score.

On an island:
When a cornerback has to cover a receiver man-to-man without help.

Pass interference:
A penalty called when the defensive player hits a receiver while a pass is in the air.

Play:
A play starts when the center snaps the ball; a play ends when the ballcarrier is tackled or goes out of bounds.

Play action:
A fake handoff to a running back before a quarterback tries to throw a pass.

Pocket:
The area where the quarterback stands to throw a pass.

Read step:
A linebacker's first step toward the line of scrimmage.

Redshirt:
Sitting out for a year to gain an extra year of eligibility for a college football player.

Sack:
When the quarterback wants to pass but is tackled behind the line of scrimmage.

Safety:
If the defense pushes the offense so far back that the ballcarrier is tackled in the end zone, the team on defense gets 2 points.

Single wing:
A formation, rarely used today, with lots of tight linemen to help run the football.

Snap count:
The number of "Hut!"s that the quarterback says before the snap.

T formation:
An offensive formation that puts the quarterback under center with three running backs behind the quarterback.

Tackle:
Making the ballcarrier fall to the ground. The offensive linemen who line up outside the guards. The defensive linemen who line up closest to the ball.

Tailgating:
Having a cookout or a party in the parking lot before a football game.

Touchback:
A kick or a punt that enters the end zone, allowing the offense to take possession on the 20-yard line.

Turnover:
An interception, or a fumble recovered by the defense, is called a turnover. This means that the defensive team gets to take over on offense.

Two-a-days:
Preseason practices that happen twice a day.

West Coast offense:
A passing offense that features short passing routes.

Wild card:
A team that makes the playoffs but didn't win its division.

YAC:
Stands for "yards after catch," the yardage that a receiver gains after he catches the ball.

APPENDIX C Puzzle Answers

FIND THE FLAG • page 9

WOOFBALL • page 15

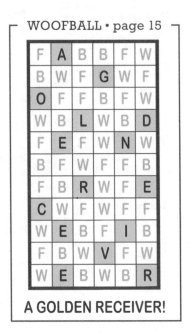

A GOLDEN RECEIVER!

WAY TO PLAY • page 19

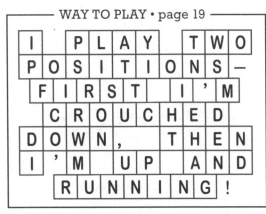

I	PLAY	TWO
POSITIONS —
FIRST	I'M
CROUCHED
DOWN,	THEN
I'M	UP	AND
RUNNING!

BRUSH UP • page 32

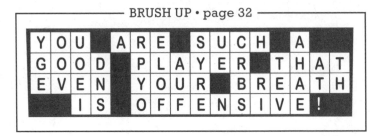

YOU ARE SUCH A
GOOD PLAYER THAT
EVEN YOUR BREATH
IS OFFENSIVE!

FIND THE FOOTBALL • page 35

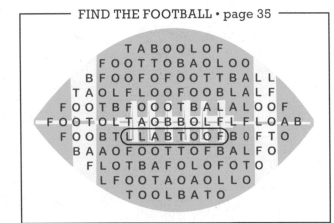

```
   TABOOLOF
  FOOTTOBAOLOO
 BFOOFOFOOTTBALL
TAOLFLOOFOOBLALF
FOOTBFOOOTBALALOOF
FOOTOLTAOBBOLFLFLOAB
FOOBT(LLABTOOF)BOFTO
BAAOFOOTTOFBALFO
 FLOTBAFOLOFOTO
  LFOOTAOAOLLO
   TOOLBATO
```

FRACTURED FOOTBALL • page 36

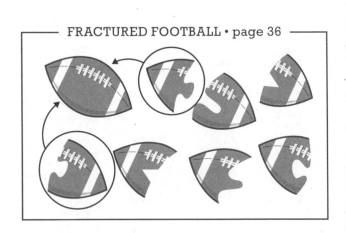

PERFECT PLAY • page 41

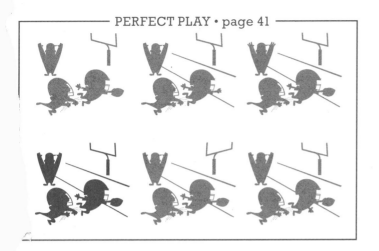

LOST PLAYER • page 47

Why did the football coach shake the vending machine?

1 H	2 E		3 W	4 A	5 N	6 T	7 E	8 D		9 H	10 I	11 S
12 Q	13 U	14 A	15 R	16 T	17 E	18 R		19 B	20 A	21 C	22 K	!

Where you wear a glove
H A N D
9 20 5 8

Opposite of loud
Q U I E T
12 13 10 2 6

Opposite of dry
W E T
3 7 16

Piece of equipment that stops a car
B R A K E
19 15 14 22 17

What happens when a car doesn't stop
C R A S H
21 18 4 11 1

FOOTBALL FILL IN • pages 50–51

SUPER SIZED • page 58

The one with the biggest head!

GO TEAM! • page 67

RAH, RAH, RAH!
SKI-U-MAH,
HOO-RAH!
HOO-RAH!
VARSITY!
VARSITY!
VARSITY,
MINN-E-SO-TAH!

TWIN TEAMMATES • page 73

WHAT'S IN A NAME? • page 68

The most popular mascots are:
EAGLES BULLDOGS TIGERS LIONS

Some more unusual mascots are:
PENGUINS KANGAROOS OWLS BLUEHENS

PEP RALLY • page 74

lunch wrappers and empty lunch bag
T R A S H

mistake in Drivers' Ed.
C R A S H

important to have in chorus
B R E A T H

art project with dried flowers
W R E A T H

what boring teachers do
P R E A C H

activity in math class
G R A P H

after-school fundraiser
C A R W A S H

WHERE'S THE PLAYER? • page 80

What is the difference between a football player and a duck?

You'll find one in a huddle, and the other in a puddle!

THE SILLY ANSWER IS... • page 82

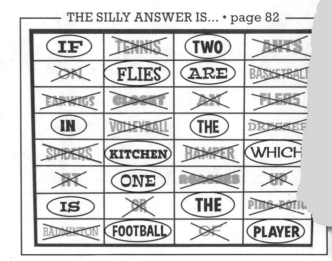

IF	~~TENNIS~~	TWO	~~ANTS~~
~~OR~~	FLIES	ARE	~~BASKETBALL~~
~~EARWIGS~~	~~CLOSET~~	~~AN~~	~~FLEAS~~
IN	~~VOLLEYBALL~~	THE	~~DRESSER~~
~~SPIDERS~~	KITCHEN	~~HAMPER~~	WHICH
~~IT~~	ONE	~~ROACHES~~	~~IS~~
IS	~~OR~~	THE	~~PING-PONG~~
~~BADMINTON~~	FOOTBALL	~~OF~~	PLAYER

HIDE THE FOOTBALL • page 87

1. Is the game on one di**sc or el**even cassettes?
2. We won! Hea**r us** "Hooray!"
3. The cham**p lay** winded in the end zone.
4. The quarterback s**pun, t**hen threw the ball.
5. Tired players **nap** before the big game.
6. Don't panic! Lo**ck** the stadium door!
7. A**ll I** need is to move the ball four more yards!
8. Losing team**s weep** in private!
9. All of Ray S**pigs' kin** came to watch him play!
10. Drinking iced **tea** makes players less thirsty.

RUN LIKE CRAZY • page 92

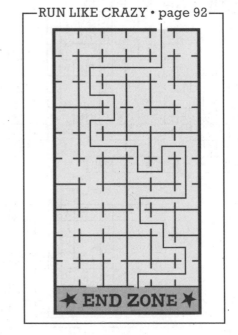

★ END ZONE ★

MOST VALUABLE PLAYER • page 101

" Hey, Coach! I want to play **END**, **GUARD**, and **TACKLE!** "

" OK — **SIT** at the **END** of the **BENCH**, **GUARD** the **WATER BUCKET**, and **TACKLE ANYONE** who gets **NEAR** it! "

WORDS TO PLAY BY • page 107

I	F		A	T		F	I	R	S	T		Y	O	U
		D	O	N	'	T		S	U	C	C	E	E	D
T	R	Y	,		T	R	Y	,		A	G	A	I	N	!

WACKY WEATHER
• page 112

BACKFIELD BUZZ • page 120

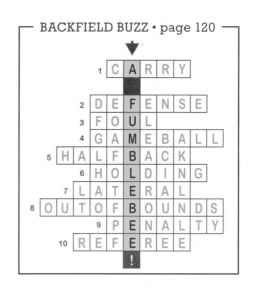

1. CARRY
2. DEFENSE
3. FOUL
4. GAMEBALL
5. HALFBACK
6. HOLDING
7. LATERAL
8. OUTOFBOUNDS
9. PENALTY
10. REFEREE
!

ALL MIXED UP • page 121

Imagine that
a fantasy
owner has players
from two
different teams.
When both "real"
teams play each
other, the
fantasy owner
will hope that
both teams
score a lot!

FANS HAVE FUN • page 122

FANCY FOOTWORK • page 127

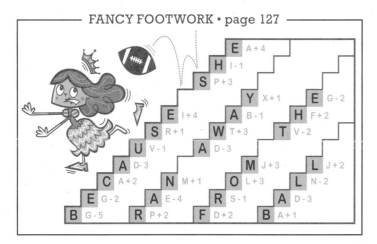

LOADS OF LAUNDRY
• page 131

Jonas __13__
Tom __16__
Jean __8__
Lonny __8__
Lida __3__

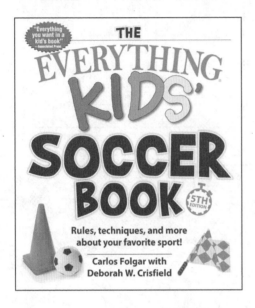
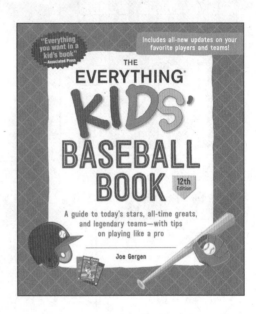
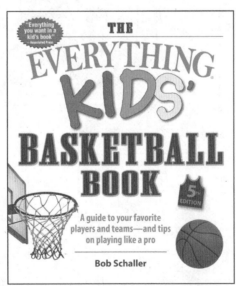